EMBELLISHING SIXTEENTH-CENTURY MUSIC

EARLY MUSIC SERIES

SERIES EDITOR
JOHN M. THOMSON

HOWARD MAYER BROWN
Embellishing Sixteenth-Century Music

JAMES BLADES AND JEREMY MONTAGU
Early Percussion Instruments

JEREMY MONTAGU
Making Early Percussion Instruments

EARLY MUSIC SERIES: 1

EMBELLISHING SIXTEENTH-CENTURY MUSIC

HOWARD MAYER BROWN

MUSIC DEPARTMENT
OXFORD UNIVERSITY PRESS
44 CONDUIT STREET, LONDON W.I.

ISBN 0 19 323175 1

2nd impression 1977

Printed in Great Britain
by The Stellar Press Hatfield
Hertfordshire

CONTENTS

NOTE

Following the most usual modern convention I have reduced the note values of the original sources by half in all the musical examples (that is, an original breve is transcribed as a semibreve, a semibreve as a minim, and so on). The following table of equivalents may help the reader to avoid confusion wherever time values are mentioned in the body of the text:

Modern	*Original*
𝅝	▯
𝅗𝅥	◇
♩	◇̩
♪	◆
𝅘𝅥𝅯	♭
𝅘𝅥𝅰	𝅘𝅥𝅯
𝅘𝅥𝅱	𝅘𝅥𝅰

INTRODUCTION

How was music in the sixteenth century actually performed? That question is difficult to answer because the music is so remote from us, both in time and in style, that even the most basic facts about the way it was played must be demonstrated rather than merely assumed. If we wish to have an accurate notion of the sound of music in the Renaissance, however, problems of performance practice must be solved, since sixteenth-century performers did not simply follow instructions given them by composers, but actively collaborated in the process of composition by determining anew, each time a piece was played, the nature of certain important details. Thus singers and instrumentalists had to know how and where to add accidentals, how to place the words under the notes in vocal music, and how to arrange compositions for effective combinations of voices and instruments, all crucial decisions that in later times became the exclusive privilege of composers.[1] In addition, sixteenth-century musicians were expected to be able to invent new melodic material extempore; they improvised either complete musical lines or sections consisting of fast passage work that could be substituted for a slower-moving written melody. And any comprehensive view of musical life in the Renaissance would be incomplete that did not take into account these spontaneous sounds.

From the Middle Ages onwards, various theorists explain the technique of adding at sight one or more contrapuntal lines to a given plainchant. Indeed, improvisation over a cantus firmus probably constituted a part of

---

[1] On the application of *musica ficta*, see the various essays by Edward E. Lowinsky, especially his foreword to H. Colin Slim, ed., *Musica Nova* (Chicago, 1964), pp. v–xxi. On the problem of text underlay in Renaissance music, see his 'A Treatise on Text Underlay by a German Disciple of Francisco de Salinas', *Festschrift Heinrich Besseler* (Leipzig, 1962), pp. 231–51, and his Introduction to Helen Hewitt, ed., *Ottaviano Petrucci, Canti B Numero Cinquanta, Venice, 1502* (Chicago, 1967), pp. v–xvi.

every musician's education, and should be considered the chief sort of unwritten music before the Baroque era.[1] Both singers and organists would frequently have had to invent counterpoint to a plainchant during liturgical services, and they might well have been asked to demonstrate this ability before being admitted into a cathedral or chapel choir.[2] And professional instrumentalists also knew how to add contrapuntal lines extempore to a given melody; *basses dances*, for example, the principal courtly dances of the fifteenth century, were normally performed by three men, two of them improvising florid melodies while the third played the pre-existent tune in long, slow notes.[3]

Musicians during the Renaissance knew, too, the technique of improvising compositions over a predetermined series of chords. These chordal patterns, most often found in the form of ostinato basses, make their first appearance in written music toward the end of the fifteenth century in the frottola and villancico repertoires, and they have a profound influence on sixteenth-century dance music.[4] But their origins may go back to the practice of early fifteenth-century Italian poet-musicians who improvised at various courts, accompanying themselves on the lute or, more charac-

---

[1] The standard work on improvisation remains Ernst T. Ferand, *Die Improvisation in der Musik* (Zurich, 1938). See also his '"Sodaine and Unexpected" Music in the Renaissance', *Musical Quarterly* 37 (1951): 10–27, and 'Improvised Vocal Counterpoint in the Late Renaissance and Early Baroque', *Annales musicologiques* 4 (1956): 129–74. Examples of written-out improvisations from the Middle Ages to the end of the nineteenth century are published in his *Die Improvisation in Beispielen aus neun Jahrhunderten abendländischer Musik* (Cologne, 1956).

[2] See, for example, Ferand, *Die Improvisation*, p. 195; and Otto Kinkeldey, *Orgel und Klavier in der Musik des 16. Jahrhunderts* (Leipzig, 1910), p. 136. Auditions for the position of organist at St. Mark's in Venice, discussed by Kinkeldey, may have involved improvising counterpoint *a 4* on a given theme, rather than adding melodic lines over a given cantus firmus. On the kinds of improvisation required of an organist in the seventeenth century, see Tobias Norlind, 'Was ein Organist im 17. Jahrhundert wissen musste', *Sammelbände der internationalen Musikgesellschaft* 7 (1905–6): 641–42.

[3] See Keith Polk, 'Flemish Wind Bands in the Late Middle Ages: A Study of Improvisatory Instrumental Practices' (Ph.D. dissertation, University of California, Berkeley, 1966). The most complete discussion of the *basse dance* is Daniel Heartz, 'The *Basse Dance*, Its Evolution circa 1450 to 1550', *Annales musicologiques* 6 (1958–63): 287–340. See also Frederick Crane, *Materials for the Study of the Fifteenth Century Basse Dance* (Brooklyn, 1968).

[4] See Otto Gombosi, 'Italia: Patria del basso ostinato', *Rassegna musicale* 7 (1934): 14–25; John Ward, 'The Folia', *Kongress-Bericht, Gesellschaft für Musikwissenschaft* (Lüneburg, 1950), pp. 94–97; and Edward E. Lowinsky, *Tonality and Atonality in Sixteenth-Century Music* (Berkeley, Calif., 1961), pp. 3–14.

teristically, the lira da braccio.[1] The latter instrument is especially adept at arpeggiated chords, and so it may well have been the playing technique of the lira that first led these men to invent harmonic patterns which were repeated over and over again as a foundation for their declamation. But the relationship between ostinato basses and the early fifteenth-century *improvvisatori* has not yet been thoroughly investigated, and so this theory about the origin of chordal patterns must remain conjectural.

Besides improvising over cantus firmi and over predetermined series of chords, musicians during the Renaissance also made up music without any fixed schemata. Free, rhapsodic flourishes on a keyboard instrument sometimes preceded more formal compositions. The crude and unpretentious keyboard preludes that survive from the fifteenth century seem to be the earliest written-out examples of this improvisatory practice; in function if not in style, these pieces are the predecessors of the often quite elaborate toccatas, preludes, and preambles of the next century, as well as of the early non-imitative ricercare.[2] Some sixteenth-century keyboard and lute players may also have been able to improvise imitative counterpoint starting from one or more germinal themes. Tomás de Sancta Maria, for example, seems to refer to some such procedure when he recommends that performers make up their own fantasias on melodic material lifted from the best vocal music,[3] and Diego Ortiz describes improvised harpsichord and viol duets not based on any pre-existent material in which the two players imitate each other, but he does not explain in detail how they coordinated their parts.[4]

---

[1] On these poet-musicians see Emile Haraszti, 'La Technique des improvisateurs de langue vulgaire et de latin au quattrocento', *Revue belge de musicologie* 9 (1955): 12–31. The best summary of information about the lira da braccio, with a complete bibliography, is Emanuel Winternitz, 'Lira da braccio', *Die Musik in Geschichte und Gegenwart* 8 (1960): cols. 935–54.

[2] These German keyboard preludes are published in Willi Apel, 'Corpus of Early Keyboard Music', vol. 1, *Keyboard Music of the Fourteenth and Fifteenth Centuries* (American Institute of Musicology, 1963), and in Bertha Wallner, ed., 'Das Erbe deutscher Musik', vols. 37–39, *Das Buxheimer Orgelbuch* (Cassel, 1958–59), nos. 58, 112, 191, 194–95, and so on.

[3] Tomás de Sancta Maria, *Libro llamado arte de tañer fantasia* (Valladolid, 1565), bk. II, chaps. 51 and 52. See also Kinkeldey, *Orgel und Klavier*, pp. 50–54. Ferand, *Die Improvisation in Beispielen*, p. 88, prints an example of such 'free' improvisation by Sancta Maria.

[4] Diego Ortiz, *Tratado de glosas sobre clausulas . . . Roma 1553*, ed. and trans. Max Schneider, 3rd rev. ed. (Cassel, 1961), pp. 35 (in German), and 51 (in Spanish). The treatise is translated into English by Peter Farrell in *Journal of the Viola da Gamba Society of America* 4 (1967): 5–9.

In short, musicians during the fifteenth and sixteenth centuries had developed a number of different techniques which enabled them to invent polyphonic music extempore. Moreover, the performing conventions of the time also allowed singers and instrumentalists to embellish, according to their own tastes, music that had already been composed — motets, madrigals, and chansons, for instance.

Sixteenth-century methods of ornamenting written music can be reconstructed with the help of ten books of instruction written in Italy between 1535 and the end of the century.[1] Four of them are by instrumentalists: Silvestro di Ganassi (1535), a viol and recorder player employed by the Basilica of San Marco in Venice as well as by the doge's court there; Diego Ortiz (1553), a Spanish viol player who was also a composer of

[1] The ten books are: Silvestro di Ganassi, *Opera intitulata Fontegara* (Venice, 1535), facsimile ed. (1934), German trans. by Hildemarie Peter (1956), and English trans. by Dorothy Swainson (1959); Diego Ortiz, *Tratado de glosas sobre clausulas . . . Roma 1553* (see p. ix, n. 4); Giovanni Camillo Maffei, *Delle lettere . . . Libri due* (Naples, 1562), 1: 3–81; the letter on singing is published in Nanie Bridgman, 'Giovanni Camillo Maffei et sa lettre sur le chant', *Revue de musicologie* 38 (1956) :3–34; Girolamo dalla Casa, *Il vero modo di diminuir*, 2 vols. (Venice, 1584), facsimile edition, Forni editore, Bologna; Giovanni Bassano, *Ricercare, Passaggi et Cadentie* (Venice, 1585); idem, *Motetti, madrigali et canzoni francese . . . diminuiti* (Venice, 1591), lost during World War II; the manuscript copy now in Hamburg, Staats- und Universitatsbibliothek, is described in Ernst T. Ferand, 'Die Motetti, Madrigali, et Canzoni Francese . . . Diminuiti . . . des Giovanni Bassano (1591)', *Festschrift Helmuth Osthoff zum 65. Geburtstage* (Tutzing, 1961), pp. 75–101; Richardo Rogniono, *Passaggi per potersi essercitare nel diminuire* (Venice, 1592); Giovanni Luca Conforto, *Breve et facile maniera d'essercitarsi ad ogni scolaro . . . a far passaggi* (Rome, 1593 [or 1603?]), facsimile ed. by Johannes Wolf (1922); Giovanni Battista Bovicelli, *Regole, passaggi di musica, madrigali e motetti passeggiati* (Venice, 1594), facsimile ed. by Nanie Bridgman (1957); and Aurelio Virgiliano, *Il Dolcimelo* (manuscript in Bologna, Civico museo bibliografico musicale, ca. 1600).

All of the volumes, except those by Maffei and Virgiliano, are listed and described in Howard Mayer Brown, *Instrumental Music printed before 1600* (Cambridge, Mass., 1965), under the appropriate years. The brief biographical notices about the various authors are taken either from the volumes themselves, or from the entries under their names in *Die Musik in Geschichte und Gegenwart*.

The standard works on improvised ornamentation in the Renaissance are Max Kuhn, *Die Verzierungs-Kunst in der Gesangs-Musik des 16.–17. Jahrhunderts (1535–1650)* (Leipzig, 1902), and Imogene Horsley, 'Improvised Embellishment in the Performance of Renaissance Polyphonic Music', *Journal of the American Musicological Society* 4 (1951): 3–19, along with the works by Ernst Ferand, listed on p. viii, n. 2. A complete list of embellishment manuals, treatises, and collections of embellished compositions from 1535 to 1688 can be found in Ernst T. Ferand, 'Didactic Embellishment Literature in the Late Renaissance: A Survey of Sources', *Aspects of Medieval and Renaissance Music*, ed. Jan La Rue (New York, 1966), pp. 154–72, which also includes alphabetical lists of composers and individual works represented in these manuals and treatises.

sacred vocal music and for fifteen years chapel master to the Duke of Alba in Naples; Girolamo Dalla Casa (1584), head of the official wind band of the Signoria of Venice; and Richardo Rogniono (1592), an instrumentalist for the governor general of Milan. Three of the instruction books are by singers: Giovanni Camillo Maffei (1562), a Neapolitan doctor, philosopher, amateur composer, and expert performer; Giovanni Luca Conforto (1593), a Roman virtuoso; and Giovanni Battista Bovicelli (1594), a member of the cathedral choir in Milan. Two are by still another Venetian, Giovanni Bassano (1585 and 1591), a composer of both vocal and instrumental music. And one is by an otherwise unknown musician, Aurelio Virgiliano (c. 1600). The books by these men are devoted principally to teaching their readers how to embellish polyphonic compositions; in addition, a number of treatises covering a broader range of subjects include more or less extensive discussions of the techniques and problems of ornamentation. The most interesting of these are by Adrian Petit Coclico (1552), Hermann Finck (1556), and Lodovico Zacconi (1592).[1] Together, these instruction books and excerpts from larger treatises constitute the primary evidence in reconstructing the practices of the sixteenth century, for they offer a clear statement of the theory of ornamentation and consequently they tell us the way musicians actually thought about what they did, as well as how they went about doing it.

Many of these writers point out that instrumentalists used exactly the same techniques to embellish compositions as singers did. Indeed, almost all the instruction books explicitly state that their examples are intended for 'ogni sorte di stromenti' as well as for 'la semplice voce'.[2] Even when a book is written with one specific instrument in mind, like Ganassi's *Fontegara* on the recorder, the author is careful to insist that his advice can

---

[1] Adrian Petit Coclico, *Compendium musices* (Nuremberg, 1552), facsimile ed. by Manfred Bukofzer (1954); Hermann Finck, *Practica musica* (Wittenberg, 1556); the chapter on singing is published in a German translation in R. Schlecht, 'Hermann Finck über die Kunst des Singens, 1556', *Monatshefte für Musikgeschichte* 11 (1879): 129–33 and 135–41; and Lodovico Zacconi, *Prattica di musica* (Venice, 1592), 2 vols., facsimile ed. (n.d.); the chapter on ornamentation is published in German translation in Friedrich Chrysander, 'Lodovico Zacconi als Lehrer des Kunstgesanges', *Vierteljahrsschrift für Musikwissenschaft* 7 (1891): 337–96.

[2] The two phrases are taken from the title page of Bassano, *Motetti* (1591). Maffei (1562) and Bovicelli (1594) are the only authors who do not mention instrumental ornamentation; while Aurelio Virgiliano alone does not mention vocal ornamentation.

be more widely applied: Ganassi's title page mentions voices as well as stringed and wind instruments, and it is illustrated with a woodcut showing a singer and three recorder players performing in a room filled with instruments — a set of viols, a lute, and two cornetti. Ganassi's attitude toward both recorder and viol playing is remarkably sophisticated; he, and other serious professional instrumentalists like him, must have been extraordinarily proficient technically. And yet he acknowledges the pre-eminent position of the human voice in the music of his time. Instruments, he writes, are inferior to voices, and he stresses again and again that an aspiring recorder player should copy the expressiveness and the melodic flexibility of a good singer, as well as the technique and style of vocal ornamentation,[1] advice that should not sound totally unfamiliar even to a twentieth-century instrumentalist.

Several instruction books – those by Juan Bermudo (1555) on all instruments, Tomás de Sancta Maria (1565) on keyboards and vihuelas, and Girolamo Diruta (1593), Hans Buchner (1551) and others on keyboards – ought also to be included among our primary theoretical evidence.[2] While they do teach basically the same techniques as the other instruction books, the keyboard manuals give us a fresh viewpoint, and including them with the other treatises on ornamentation helps to put sixteenth-century techniques in historical perspective, since the only treatises from the fifteenth century to give detailed information about the practice of ornamentation are the several keyboard *fundamenta* by German

---

[1] Ganassi, *Fontegara*, chaps. 1, 2, 13, 23, 24, 25.

[2] Juan Bermudo, *El libro llamado declaracion de instrumentos musicales* (Ossuna, 1555), facsimile ed. by Macario Santiago Kastner (1957); Sancta Maria, *Libro llamado arte de tañer fantasia*, and Girolamo Diruta, *Il Transilvano* (Venice, 1593), are all described in Brown, *Instrumental Music*, under the appropriate years. A part of the Bermudo treatise is summarized in Kinkeldey, *Orgel und Klavier*, pp. 9–25; a part of the Sancta Maria treatise is also summarized there, pp. 25–55, and eight chapters translated into German in Tomás de Sancta Maria, *Wie mit aller Vollkommenheit und Meisterschaft das Klavichord Isicl zu spielen sei*, trans. Richard Boadella and Eta Harich-Schneider (Cassel, 1937) Some of the Diruta treatise is translated and the entire volume summarized in Carl Krebs' 'Girolamo Diruta's Transilvano', *Vierteljahrsschrift für Musikwissenschaft* 8 (1892): 307–88.

On the Hans Buchner treatise, see Carl Paesler, 'Fundamentbuch von Hans von Constanz', *Vierteljahrsschrift für Musikwissenschaft* 5 (1889): 1–192, esp. p. 33, where the mordent is described by Buchner and his usage is compared with that of other German musicians.

organists.[1] Thus these furnish continuity and a basis for comparison with the more abundant sixteenth-century material. Symbols for so-called mordents, for example, are explained both in fifteenth- and sixteenth-century books on keyboard technique; since such symbols appear in music for the keyboard as early as the fourteenth century[2] and do not regularly appear in any other kind of late medieval or Renaissance music, their existence is an important piece of evidence about the practice of ornamentation that could not otherwise be known.

If treatises on keyboard technique can help us to discover how both vocal and instrumental ensemble music was embellished, then surely the entire corpus of lute and keyboard music from the sixteenth century must also be taken into account, for much of that repertoire consists of intabulations of vocal music, chansons, madrigals, motets, and masses, presented in more or less highly embellished versions.[3] Indeed, most of the great lute virtuosi of the century, men like Francesco da Milano, Pietro Paolo Borrono, and Alberto da Ripa, made their reputations as much because they were great performers of other men's music, which means that they were skilful at embellishing, as because they were great composers of fantasias and dances. The volumes of music published by these men are thus the closest thing to phonograph records that we shall ever have from the sixteenth century, for they preserve personal, idiosyncratic versions of well-known compositions as they were performed by leading sixteenth-century virtuosi. Alfred Einstein has challenged the authority of the books devoted principally to embellishment on the grounds that the florid extravagances of their examples are more easily explained as pedagogical excess than as normal usage.[4] But the corpus of lute and keyboard music increases many times the some 125 actual compositions included as

---

[1] See, for example, the *fundamena* published in Apel, *Keyboard Music*, pp. 13, 20–23, and so on.

[2] If the circles above some notes in the Robertsbridge Codex, published in Apel, pp. 1–9, do in fact designate mordents. If they do not, then the earliest sources to use such symbols are the fifteenth-century German keyboard pieces published by Apel, and the *Buxheimer Orgelbuch*.

[3] The entire corpus of printed lute and keyboard music is listed and described in Brown, *Instrumental Music*. For an attempt to survey ornamentation in some sixteenth-century lute music, see H. M. Brown, 'Embellishment in Early Sixteenth-Century Italian Intabulations,' *Proceedings of the Royal Musical Association* 100 (1973–4): 49–84.

[4] Alfred Einstein, *The Italian Madrigal*, 3 vols. (Princeton, N.J. 1949) 1: 227.

examples in these embellishment manuals,[1] and this more abundant repertoire serves as a responsible check on the reliability of sixteenth-century
teachers of ornamentation. Lute and keyboard music not only shows us
how musicians actually did ornament what they played; it also reveals the
kinds of music normally subjected to embellishment, as well as the way
tastes changed during the century. In short, all the evidence — embellishment books, general theoretical treatises as well as those devoted to
keyboard instruments alone, and the huge body of polyphonic music
arranged for instrumental soloists — must be taken into account before a
coherent picture of the·normal conventions of performance during the
sixteenth century can emerge.

[1] And all listed in Ferand, 'Didactic Embellishment Literature'.

I

SIXTEENTH-CENTURY GRACES

Most writers on embellishments, both during the Renaissance and in the present century, agree that sixteenth-century performers normally ornamented written music by applying running figuration patterns, so-called diminutions, *passaggi*, or *gorgie*, to a basic melody;[1] that is, they substituted for the longer notes or groups of notes in a composition (the breves, semibreves, and sometimes even minims) fast-moving stereotyped melodic formulas to produce what was in effect a melodic variation. But almost all the sixteenth-century authors also make a distinction between specific ornaments applied to single notes — ornaments that can conveniently be called 'graces', although that name was never applied to them in the sixteenth century — as opposed to longer, freer, running passages that substitute for the slower-moving basic intervals of a melody — ornaments that can conveniently be called diminutions or *passaggi*, as they normally were called during most of the century.[2]

This distinction is implicit in Martin Agricola's statement as early as 1528 that all instrumentalists must learn how to decorate their performances the way organists do, with 'Coloriren' or 'Coloratur', that is, *passaggi*, as

---

[1] Variants of the terms *diminutions* and *passaggi* appear in all of the theoretical literature cited. The word *gorgia*, used to mean vocal ornamentation, first appears in Nicola Vicentino, *L'antica musica ridotta alla moderna prattica* (Rome, 1555), facsimile ed. by Edward E. Lowinsky (1959), bk. IV, chap. 42, p. 88 (recte 94). Ganassi refers to the throat ('gorgia', or in Venetian dialect 'gorza') and its role in ornamentation. *Gorgia* seems to be a term restricted to vocal embellishment, while the others can be used interchangeably, for vocal or instrumental embellishments.

[2] This terminology was suggested to me by Robert Donington, *The Interpretation of Early Music* (London, 1963), p. 96.

well as 'Mordanten', that is, graces.[1] Although Ganassi devotes almost his entire treatise on the recorder to *passaggi*, he does say near the end of it that the easiest ornaments of all are *tremoli*, by which he means the grace that we would call trill or mordent.[2] Diego Ortiz seems to say the same thing in advising viol players to mix some 'quiebros amortiguados', muted trills, among their 'passos', or *passaggi*.[3] And with varying degrees of clarity and detail authors throughout the rest of the century continue to divide ornaments into these two separate but related categories.

Most of the graces described in the sixteenth-century treatises are shown in Example 1. Two of them, the *tremolo* and the *groppo*, seem to have been in common use throughout the entire century, while the remaining seven are mentioned only by one or two writers, or else were introduced late in the century and became a part of the standard vocabulary of early seventeenth-century embellishment. Four of the nine graces are taken from the table prepared in 1593 by Girolamo Diruta for keyboard players,[4] and I have adopted his terminology, which seems, in fact, to be the standard one. He is more analytical than most sixteenth-century musicians in dividing diminutions into five classes: *minuta* (by which he means *passaggi*), *tremoli*, *groppi*, *clamationi*, and *accenti*. He has, in other words, gone further than earlier writers in isolating and defining a variety of ornaments that can be applied to single notes, and in giving each one of them a specific name. This process of ever greater refinement in the invention and classification of graces, which distinguishes later from earlier sixteenth-century musicians, was, of course, to continue, and results finally in those elaborate tables of graces added to so many seventeenth- and eighteenth-century treatises and collections of music.[5] My table is but a rudimentary version of those later and more detailed collections of turns and trills.

---

[1] Martin Agricola, *Musica instrumentalis deudsch* (Wittenberg, 1529; 2nd ed., 1545), quasi-facsimile ed. by Robert Eitner, *Publikation älterer praktischer und theoretischer Musikwerke* 20 (1896): 222.

[2] Ganassi, *Fontegara*, chap. 24.

[3] Ortiz, *Tratado* (1961 ed.), p. 5 and, in German, p. xxix.

[4] Diruta, *Il Transilvano*, bk. I, p. 20, and bk. II, p. 13.

[5] See, for example, the composite table in Robert Donington, 'Ornaments', *Grove's Dictionary of Music and Musicians*, 5th ed. (London, 1954) 6: 441–48.

Example 1   Sixteenth - Century Graces

(a)
TREMOLO
(Diruta, 1593, I, p. 20)

(Sancta Maria, 1565, fol. 48, called 'quiebros')

(b)

GROPPO (Diruta, 1593, II, p. 13)

(Conforto, 1593, p. 25)

or

(c)
SPECIAL TREMOLO
('Quiebros de minimas')
(Sancta Maria. 1565, fol. 47ᵛ)

(d)
REDOBLE
(loc. cit.)

(e) **TREMOLO GROPPIZATO**
(Dalla Casa, 1584,1, p.5)

(f)
GROPPO BATTUTO
(Dalla Casa, 1584,1, p.6)

(g) **TRILLO**
(Conforto, 1593,p.25)

(h)
CLAMATIONE
(Diruta, 1593, II, p.13)

(i)
ACCENTO
(loc. cit.)

The *tremolo* can be defined as a rapid alternation between a main note and its upper or lower auxiliary. The interval between the two notes can be a half step, a whole step, or a third, and it can be repeated once, twice, or many times, either in measured or, perhaps more normally, in unmeasured units of time, but apparently a *tremolo* seldom took up more than half of the time value of the main note.[1] Thus it combines the two graces that we more usually call the trill and the mordent. In fact, 'mordent' is the term applied to the *tremolo* in German theoretical literature, and its use is prescribed by symbols, usually a hook drawn from a notehead, in a good deal of fifteenth- and sixteenth-century German keyboard music.[2]

Symbols to mark the notes to which *tremoli* should be added are extremely rare outside German keyboard music. So far as I know they do not appear in any sixteenth-century music for voices or for instrumental ensemble. Several volumes of lute music indicate *tremoli*, by signs especially invented in each case. Vicenzo Capirola in his manuscript anthology of about 1517 uses dotted red numbers to identify the upper auxiliary which is to be repeated, and two dots above the number of the fret for the grace he calls 'tremolo s'un tasto solo' (a *tremolo* on one fret), by which he means a mordent, usually alternating between the first fret and the open string.[3] And in the 1548 Milanese edition of Pietro Paolo Borrono's music, the anonymous editor inserts parentheses to isolate the two notes of a *tremolo*.[4] While these two examples hardly constitute

---

[1] Ganassi, *Fontegara*, chaps. 24 and 25; Bermudo, *Instrumentos musicales*, bk. IV, chap. 2; Sancta Maria, *Arte de tañer fantasia* bk. I, chap. 19; and Diruta, *Il Transilvano*, bk. I, pp. 18–21, furnish the most detailed description of the *tremolo*. Only Ganassi discusses *tremoli* in thirds. Sancta Maria writes that his trill (Example 1a) can also be played beginning on the note above the final note but with the accompanying chord struck with the second note (i.e. the trill begins with an anticipatory upper appoggiatura).

[2] See, for example, Willi Apel, *The Notation of Polyphonic Music, 900–1600*, 4th ed. (Cambridge, Mass., 1953), pp. 24 and 30; and also the music published in Apel, *Keyboard Music*. Antonio Valente, *Intavolatura de cimbalo* (Naples, 1576), repr. Oxford, 1973, ed. Charles Jacobs, described in Brown, *Instrumental Music*, as 1576_3, indicates a grace by placing the letter *t* above a note.

[3] See Otto Gombosi, ed., *Compositione di Meser Vincenzo Capirola* (Neuilly-sur-Seine, 1955), pp. x–xi, xxvi, xc–xci, and Compositions 13–16.

[4] See Daniel Heartz, 'Les premières "instructions" pour le luth', in *Le Luth et sa musique*, ed. Jean Jacquot (Paris, 1958), pp. 85–87. The Borrono volume is described in Brown as 1548_3. For more information on graces in lute music, see Diana Poulton, 'Graces of play in renaissance lute music', *Early Music* 3 (1975): 107–14.

overwhelming proof of a ubiquitous convention, nevertheless their evidence, weighed with the rest, strongly suggests that *tremoli* may be applied to music for lute as well as for keyboard.

Ganassi furnishes the most detailed information about the way this grace was played by other instruments. He supplies a table of *tremoli* for almost every note on the recorder, and explains that those that move by half step are sweet and soothing ('suave over placabile'), and those that move by thirds are lively ('vivace'), while whole-step *tremoli* have neutral ('mediocre') expressive value.[1] But, though he writes that they are the simplest embellishments, he offers no advice about where to add them in a composition, nor, indeed, about precisely how to play them.

Ganassi is not the only writer to convey the impression that *tremoli* are the easiest of all ornaments to perform. The keyboard teachers Tomás de Sancta Maria and Girolamo Diruta, whose explanations of the grace are by far the most detailed, both imply the same thing, since they discuss them early in their treatises and only later introduce the more complex subject of diminutions proper.[2] They both seem to suggest, then, that a beginning harpsichordist or organist learned how to add *tremoli* early in his training, long before he was ready to master the more virtuoso and demanding *passaggi*. Zacconi, writing about singers in 1592, clearly and explicitly gives that advice. 'The *tremolo*,' he says, 'is the true door for entering into *passaggi*, and for mastering *gorgie*; for a ship moves more easily once it has been set in motion than when it must begin to move at the start of its journey.'[3]

If *tremoli* are the easiest of ornaments to play, perhaps, then, they were the graces most often added to sixteenth-century music. At least one sixteenth-century musician, the Spaniard Juan Bermudo, would tolerate

---

[1] Ganassi, *Fontegara*, chaps. 24 and 25. He also explains that the pitches of some *tremoli* deviate slightly from the correct ones, a fact which seems not to bother him. In truth, his trill fingerings are effective on modern reproductions of sixteenth-century recorders, although they are slightly out of tune.

[2] Whereas Sancta Maria discusses *tremoli* in *Arte de tañer fantasia*, bk. I, chap. 19, he explains *passaggi* in chap. 23. Diruta, *Il Transilvano*, bk. I, pp. 18–21, deals with *tremoli* and *groppi*, and bk. II, pp. 10–14, with *passaggi*.

[3] *Prattica di musica*, bk. I, chap. 66, fol. 60: '. . . il tremolo, cioè la voce tremante è la vera porta d'intrar dentro a passaggi, & di impataonirse delle gorgie: perche con piu facilità se ne và la Nave quando che prima è mossa; che quando nel principio la si vuol movere . . .'

no others.[1] And in any case, the amount of evidence, and the fact that it applies to instruments as well as to voices and comes from every decade in the century, should encourage us to believe that the *tremolo* was commonly added to all sorts of music between 1500 and 1600. Sancta Maria and Diruta are the only writers to attempt to explain where and how it should be used; and their directions are scarcely specific. Sancta Maria writes that *tremoli* can decorate semibreves, minims, and occasionally semiminims.[2] And Diruta advises the player to add them at the beginnings of ricercari, canzoni, and other pieces, when one hand plays only a single line, and wherever else they appear to be convenient or appropriate. He does give a number of examples of *tremoli* which he adds to scale fragments of various speeds, and to semiquaver (*crome*) passage work (Example 2);

Example 2
(Diruta, I, 21)
Plain:

With tremoli:

and he praises Claudio Merulo for his particularly skilful use of the grace, citing as a typical example of Merulo's more complex *tremoli* the passage shown in Example 3, which he warns the inexperienced player against attempting.[3]

But indeed, Diruta's advice, to add *tremoli* wherever they are convenient or appropriate, that is, wherever the performer with taste wishes, seems to be borne out by the music itself, for *tremoli* are sprinkled liberally through-

---

[1] *Instrumentos musicales*, bk. IV, chap. 43, fol. 84v–85. See also Kinkeldey, *Orgel und Klavier*, pp. 22–23.

[2] *Arte de tañer fantasia*, bk. I, chap. 19.
Diruta, *Il Transilvano*, bk. I, pp. 20–22, and, in German translation, in Krebs' 'Diruta's Transilvano', p. 341.

out those German keyboard compositions which note them,[1] and in a number of pieces both in the Capirola and the Borrono lute books. It would be impossible to formulate a general rule about the use of *tremoli*,

Example 3

(Diruta, I, 20)

for example, on the basis of this Padoana by Capirola (Example 4),[2] let alone a rule accounting for the difference between *tremoli* with upper and those with lower auxiliaries, which Capirola, exceptionally, is so careful to mark. After the opening few measures, Capirola adds no further graces in this piece; clearly the performer, having been shown the way, can put others wherever his instincts tell him and the technique of his instrument allows.

The function of the *groppo*, the other grace most commonly used throughout the whole century, was much more clearly defined than that of the *tremolo*, for the *groppo* is nothing more than a cadential trill on the subsemitone, usually starting on the upper note, that is, the tonic. As Example 1b shows, the subsemitone could, however, be held for a time before the *groppo* actually began, and the ornament usually ended with a formula involving the underthird. Sometimes *groppi* are introduced or quitted by more elaborate formulas, and often they get progressively faster as they near resolution. In fact, even in the sixteenth century, cadential trills may often have been genuinely unmeasured. Although Zacconi speaks of *semicrome* (demisemiquavers in the musical examples), he

---

[1] For the fifteenth-century sources, see n. 2, page ix; for some sixteenth-century sources, see Apel, *Notation*, pp. 24 and 30, and also Krebs, 'Diruta's Transilvano', pp. 368–70.

[2] Gombosi, 'Italia', pp. 43 ff.

does say that the two notes of a *groppo* can be repeated as often as the time allows.[1] And Dalla Casa implies the existence of unmeasured *groppi* by labelling one of his special graces 'groppo battuto', that is, measured trill.[2] Dalla Casa, whose treatise dates from 1584, is the earliest writer known to me actually to use the term *groppo*; it was apparently invented only late

Example 4

(Gombosi, *Compositione di meser Vincenzo Capirola*, p.43f)

etc.

---

[1] *Prattica di musica*, bk. I, chap. 66, fol. 62ᵛ, and, in German, in Chrysander, '*Zacconi als Lehrer*', p. 361.

[2] *Il vero modo*, pp. 6–7.

in the century.[1] And yet cadential trills appear so frequently in all of the embellished music throughout the century that we should not hesitate to add them even to compositions written long before any special name was given to them.

The remaining graces found in Example 1 ought to be handled with greater care. Sancta Maria's special trill and *redoble*, Dalla Casa's *groppo battuto* and *tremolo groppizato*, and Diruta's *accento* were almost certainly employed by other performers, but they were not usual enough graces to dignify with a commonly accepted name. Diruta's *clamationi* and Conforto's *trillo*, on the other hand, are described and named by other writers. But both of these graces seem to have been introduced into music very late in the sixteenth century; they reflect early Baroque tastes; and, in fact, they both became standard ornaments in early seventeenth-century music. The *clamatione*, a slide or portamento up to an initial note in a phrase from the third or fourth below, first described as a keyboard ornament, was extensively used by Bovicelli in 1594 as a vocal embellishment, although he did not label it with any specific descriptive term. Such slides were already considered somewhat old hat by Caccini in 1601;[2] he spoke enthusiastically, on the other hand, about the *trillo*, a controlled vibrato on one note which normally gathered speed as it neared completion.[3] The,

[1] The term also appears in Conforto, *Breve et facile maniera*, p. 25; and Bovicelli, *Regole*, p. 11 as well as in Diruta, *Il Transilvano*, as we have seen.

[2] Giulio Caccini, *Le Nuove musiche* (Florence, 1601), p. 6, and, in English translation, in Oliver Strunk, *Source Readings in Music History* (New York, 1950), p. 382. See also the complete edition of *Le nuove musiche*, ed. H. Wiley Hitchcock (Madison, Wisconsin, 1970), which includes an English translation of the preface.

[3] Caccini, p. 7, writes that, in order to perform a *trillo*, it is necessary to 'ribattere ciascuna nota con la gola sopra la vocale, à, sino all'ultima breve', which Strunk, p. 384, following John Playford's seventeenth-century version, translates as 'to beat every note with the throat upon the vowel *a* unto the last breve'. According to Strunk, p. 391, Playford observes that a *trillo* is 'the shaking of the uvula or palate on the throat *in one sound upon a note*' (italics mine) and that it can be imitated by beating or shaking a finger on the singer's throat while he is singing one note. Moreover, Girolamo Fantini, *Modo per imparare a sonare di tromba* (Frankfurt, 1638; facsimile ed., Milan, 1934), p. 6, says that a trumpeter attacks a *trillo* with his chest rather than his tongue, and beats each note with his throat ('il trillo và fatto a forza di petto, e battuto con la gola') and on p. 11 he gives examples of *trilli* in which the player produces the ornament by repeating the vowels *a*, *e*, *i*, or *o*. Thus the ornament ought to be a controlled vibrato rather than the ugly and awkward series of newly articulated repeated notes perpetrated by so many twentieth-century singers as *trilli*.

Christopher Simpson, *The Division-Viol* (London, 1659), facsimile of 2nd ed., 1665 (London, 1955), p. 12, recommends that viol players use 'gruppi', *trilli*, and all other vocal ornaments. Although he writes that such ornaments should be played in a single bow, he does not explain how a *trillo* can be performed in that manner.

trillo, apparently one of the glories of late Renaissance and early Baroque singers, may be the earliest example of an idiomatically conceived ornament: it is specifically intended for the human voice alone and, indeed, it can scarcely be imitated satisfactorily on any instrument, although some Baroque instrumentalists did attempt it.[1] In short, *clamationi* and *trilli* ought to be reserved for music written, or at any rate performed, after 1590. And the special graces described by only one or two writers ought not to be used indiscriminately. But we may add *tremoli* and *groppi* and no other kinds of ornaments to virtually any composition written during the sixteenth century with some confidence that we are not violating any but the most flamboyant and the most conservative of Renaissance tastes. The superius of Jacques Arcadelt's madrigal 'O felici occhi miei', for instance, might well have been embellished only with graces in the manner shown in Example 5A (see next page).[2]

[1] See, for example, Fantini, n.3, page 10.

[2] The superius is taken from Ortiz, *Tratado de glosas*, pp. 69–72. I have differentiated among mordents (indicated by ⤻), trills (beginning on the main note and indicated by *tr*), and trills by thirds (beginning on the main note and indicated by *3*). *Groppi* are indicated by the signs ⌐ ⌐ . The full brackets refer to Example 5c, discussed below.

Example 5 Arcadelt, 'O felici occhi miei'
  A. With Tremoli and Groppi
  (✳ = mordent; *tr* = modern trill, begining on main note; *3* = trill by a third.)

B. Embellished by Ortiz (1553)

C. Embellished from Ganassi's tables

[14]

SIXTEENTH-CENTURY *PASSAGGI*

Graces on single notes by no means exhaust the possibilities of freedom allowed to sixteenth-century performers in embellishing music. The authors of the ornamentation manuals concentrate mainly on *passaggi*; they devote most of their space to explaining how to break up the longer notes of a composition by applying to them stereotyped melodic formulas made up of many short notes. This basic technique of appliquéing pre-formed figuration patterns onto a given melody did not change during the century, and, indeed, almost all the instruction books teach the subject in the same way. The authors present a series of systematic tables showing alternative melodic formulas for each of the most common intervals, ascending and descending seconds, thirds, fourths, fifths, and, toward the end of the century, sixths, sevenths, and octaves as well. In addition, most authors include examples of multiple ways to decorate cadences and also a few standard melodic figures of the sort that appear in almost every composition, such as scale fragments. In a manuscript appendix to one copy of Ganassi's *Fontegara* (1535), the author himself added 175 variants to a single cadential formula[1] — he had, in fact, promised 300 — but most authors are content with less than 20 different embellishments for each interval. A comparison of Ortiz's 12 relatively simple ways of decorating a semibreve that ascends a second[2] (Example 6) with Bovicelli's 35 ornate alternatives for the same interval[3] (Example 7), gives some concrete notion

---

[1] Modern edition in Ganassi, *Fontegara*, English and German translations, pp. 97–104.

[2] Ortiz, *Tratado*, p. 41.

[3] Bovicelli, *Regole*, pp. 17–18.

Example 6 Ortiz's embellishments for an ascending second

Example 7 Bovicelli's embellishments for an ascending second

of the extremes of complexity to be found in the sixteenth-century theoretical literature. These ornaments and the others like them were presumably to be practised and learned by rote, so that each performer would have an instant supply of clichés that could be added on the spot to any composition.

Even though all teachers of ornamentation presented their subject matter by means of systematic tables of intervals, individual writers did nevertheless arrange the material in slightly different ways, revealing their own idiosyncrasies and special emphases. The tables published by Diego Ortiz, for instance, as well as the more random samples of diminutions included in treatises by Coclico, Finck, and Maffei, all include a much higher proportion of cadential formulas than of simple intervals. It is clear from this emphasis as well as from the fact that cadences are invariably singled out as a special category by all writers, that *passaggi* may always be added to cadences, even when no other embellishment seems warranted, although no sixteenth-century evidence quite suggests that all cadences ought to be decorated, as many seventeenth- and eighteenth-century writers say.[1]

Diego Ortiz presents *passaggi* that are simpler than anyone else's, for reasons which will become clear below, and his book is for that reason the best starting point for anyone interested in learning this obsolete art. But Ortiz gives three separate tables for each interval, depending on whether its two notes are breves, semibreves, or minims, whereas Ganassi writes all the basic intervals as semibreves, explains how his ornaments can be played if the basic notes are breves or minims, and indicates that his examples can be transformed from duple to triple time.[2] Moreover, Ganassi presents a number of variant forms even of the basic intervals, so that the same *passaggi* as apply to an ascending second, for example, can also be used for a number of other melodic fragments. That is, all the basic forms shown in Example 8 can be ornamented by *passaggi* which are in the first place intended for an ascending second in semibreves.[3] As Imogene Horsley has pointed out,[4] Ganassi's use of alternative forms for all the basic intervals implies that he conceived of these intervals as occurring from semibreve to semibreve. That is, a musician wishing to follow Ganassi's advice in decorating a melody should first designate as the basic intervals the distance between the notes which begin each half-bar and ignore the intervening notes. Thus in the phrase from Arcadelt's 'O felici occhi miei' shown in Example 9A, the second and fourth minims of each measure should be ignored and ornaments for the basic intervals shown in Example 9B should be chosen from Ganassi's tables. Ornaments applied in

---

[1] On obligatory ornaments during the Baroque era, and especially cadential trills, see Donington, *Interpretation of Early Music*, pp. 125–26 and 171.

[2] Ganassi, chaps. 13 and 18–22. His rather scholastic division of diminutions in chaps. 10–12 according to the time values of individual notes, the melodic patterns, and the rhythmic proportions, of little practical value, is summarized in Horsley, 'Improvised Embellishment', p. 6.

[3] Ganassi, English and German translations, pp. 20–21, and see his discussion of the variants in chap. 18.

[4] Horsley, pp. 7–8.

Example 8   Motives that can be embellished like ascending seconds
             according to Ganassi.

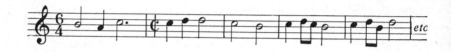

etc

Example 9

A. A phase from Arcadelt, 'O felici occhi miei'.

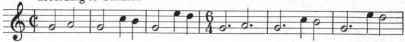

B. Its 'basic intervals'

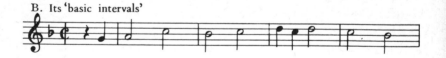

A.

B.

this way have a certain freedom from the shape of the original melody that sixteenth-century taste apparently appreciated. And this freedom is explicitly acknowledged by Ganassi; although he admonishes his readers to begin and end their *passaggi* on the main note of the melody so that the counterpoint will still be correct as composed, he does allow exceptions — stepwise motion to fill in larger intervals, for example, and syncopations — and ornamenting from semibreve to semibreve will necessitate still others.[1] Once exceptions are admitted and *passaggi* are quitted by a note other than the original one, some contrapuntal barbarisms will almost invariably creep in. But Ganassi, and most of the other teachers of ornamentation as well, felt that an occasional untoward dissonance or parallel fifth or octave was a price worth paying for a particularly brilliant effect.[2] And in any case, as Ganassi and others stress, such barbarisms pass so quickly when they are a part of fast-moving *passaggi* that even the most learned of listeners can scarcely hear them at all.

But the most distinctive feature of Ganassi's *Fontegara* is the fact that it includes four complete tables of ornaments, the first in normal mensuration, the second in units of five semiminims to be played in the time of four, the third in units of six semiminims in the time of four, and the fourth in units of seven semiminims in the time of four. Ganassi's way of handling these proportions is demonstrated in Example 10, where *passaggi* for the same interval from all four tables are juxtaposed.[3] No other teacher of ornamentation discusses proportions,[4] let alone those in ratios of 5:4, 6:4, and 7:4; thus Ganassi's insistence on this much rhythmic complexity seems at first a manifestation of a particularly scholastic turn of mind, or at least of an excess of pedagogical zeal. But in fact these elaborate proportional tables do not reflect a finicky and overly theoretical regard

---

[1] Ganassi, chap. 13.

[2] See Ganassi, chap. 13; Ortiz, *Tratado de glosas*, p. 6, and, in German, p. xxx; Finck, ed. Schlecht, 'Finck über die Kunst des Singens', p. 141; and Rogniono, *Passaggi*, bk. II, fol. CIᵛ.

[3] Ganassi, English and German translations, pp. 20, 40, 60, and 80.

[4] But Rogniono, bk. I, p. 13, does include some exercises with ten *crome* (quavers) to the semibreve.

for polymetric combinations so much as they reveal Ganassi's predilection for free rhythms, completely sprung from their metrical straitjacket, for these *passaggi* must have been played so fast that they sounded virtually unmeasured rather than extraordinarily carefully measured. Even in

Example 10   Ornaments from Ganassi's four tables

Ganassi's first set of tables some *passaggi* are written in apparently complex rhythms[1] (see Example 11); but given the speed at which such figures had to be played, they must represent an attempt to fix improvisatory freedoms in writing. And the examples in normal mensuration confirm the impression that his second, third, and fourth tables are merely a systematic effort

1 Ganassi, English and German translations, pp. 20–21.

to capture on paper the rhythmic licences that he allowed himself in performance. In other words, far from insisting on Gothic intricacy Ganassi in 1535 was attempting to explain the same sort of sprung rhythms that Zacconi, writing in 1592, describes as a characteristic feature of improvised embellishment.[1] Zacconi says that many excellent singers give

Example 11   Ganassi, table 1, excerpts

their listeners great pleasure even though their embellishments contain fewer or more notes than the proper number, which he fixes at eight to the tactus, that is, *crome* (semiquavers in the musical examples). He might well have expressed the same idea by saying that these virtuosi sing in proportions of 5:4, 6:4, or 7:4. If the singers know how to adapt these extra notes to the prevailing metre, and sing them in time, Zacconi continues, even expert musicians will not object or even notice, unless they see them written down. And in another passage from the same treatise,[2] Zacconi concludes that it is better to learn diminutions by ear rather than by written example, since the correct rhythms ('misura et tempo') are impossible to transcribe correctly. Like twentieth-century jazz, then, the rhythm of which looks immensely complicated when it is written down accurately, at least a part of the published *passaggi* from the sixteenth century, and notably those by Ganassi, are an attempt to capture in print the essentially free rhythmic style of some improvisations.

Even though the presence of irregular groupings by fives, sixes, and sevens distinguishes Ganassi's ornamentation manual from all the others

[1] See Zacconi, *Prattica di musica*, bk. I, chap. 66, fol. 62v, and, in German, in Chrysander, 'Lodovico Zacconi', p. 360.

[2] Zacconi, bk. I, chap. 66, fol. 58, and, in German, in Chrysander, p. 342.

in the sixteenth century, nevertheless many of his *passaggi*, even those involving an irregular number of notes, proceed in evenly flowing semiminims (quavers in the musical examples), *crome* (semiquavers), and *semicrome* (demisemiquavers). Almost all of Ortiz's diminutions move in even *crome* (semiquavers) with a few semiminims (quavers), and even fewer *semicrome* (demisemiquavers in the musical examples). Indeed, one of the characteristic traits of *passaggi* throughout the century is their tendency to proceed in stepwise motion and equal time values, with simple rhythmic patterns and occasional skips introduced for the sake of variety. Obviously the smaller the note values the more difficult it becomes either to play or to comprehend complex rhythms. And while Ganassi and Ortiz both write diminutions that move quickly, musicians from the last two decades of the sixteenth century concentrate even more on speed. Dalla Casa's tables of ornamented intervals are divided not only by the length of the basic intervals, whether semibreve or minim in the original notation, but also by the speed of the *passaggi*, whether *crome* (semiquavers, eight to one of the original semibreves), *semicrome* (demisemiquavers, sixteen to one of the original semibreves), or what he calls *treplicate* (demi-semiquaver triplets, twenty-four to one of the original semibreves) and *quadruplicate* (hemidemisemiquavers, thirty-two to one of the original semibreves). He does not even mention semiminims (quavers in the musical examples), which he calls *semplici*, among the note values suitable for diminutions, although he does include some among his earlier examples. He is surprised, he writes, that no one before him has discussed *treplicate* and *quadruplicate*;[1] they are both necessary for ornamenting, since 'il vero modo di diminuir' consists in mixing notes of all four lengths.

Dalla Casa may be guilty of a slight exaggeration in insisting on demi-semiquaver triplets and hemidemisemiquavers as an absolutely essential ingredient in an acceptably embellished part, for Zacconi, whose advice is among the most sensible and musically sound of the whole century, explains — a bit apologetically, to be sure — that he has not included any *passaggi* in hemidemisemiquavers because he is writing for students and not for those who already know how to improvise embellishments.[2]

---

[1] Dalla Casa, *Il vero modo*, bk. I, fol. A2.

[2] Zacconi, bk. I, chap. 66, fol. 76, and, in German, in Chrysander, p. 395.

Anyone who has mastered demisemiquavers, he continues, can learn to play hemidemisemiquavers by halving the time value of his examples. Clearly hemidemisemiquavers, at least so far as Zacconi was concerned, were reserved for the most accomplished, or most exhibitionistic, of virtuosi. On the other hand, virtuoso singers in the sixteenth century actually did include such rapid notes among their embellishments; some are to be found, for example, in the music performed by Vittoria Archilei and Jacopo Peri at the festivities celebrating the marriage of Ferdinando de'Medici and Christine of Lorraine in Florence in 1589, several years after Dalla Casa's treatise was published.[1] And hemidemisemiquavers also appear in the books on ornamentation by Bassano, Rogniono, and Bovicelli, in short, in all the embellishment treatises of the 1580s and 1590s except the one by Giovanni Luca Conforto, who may well have used them, for he, like Zacconi before him, explains that the time values of all his examples can be halved if the performer so desires.

By the time these last four instruction books of the century were published, the manner of presenting the subject of diminutions had become traditional, and the chief interest of the volumes lies in the copious examples of actual compositions embellished by the various authors. The only distinctive feature of Bassano's short treatise of 1585 is that it opens, like the second volume of Ortiz's book of 1553, with a collection of monophonic ricercari, for recorder, viol, cornetto, or other single-line instruments, intended to demonstrate the technique of improvising similar pieces but also designed to introduce the student to the style and principal technical problems of embellishing music that was already composed.[2] Richardo Rogniono in 1592 teaches this preliminary matter more systematically in writing half of his short instruction book as a series of finger exercises, scales, combinations of seconds and thirds, thirds and fourths, and diminution figures, which are to be practised sequentially, up and

---

[1] See the modern edition of this music, *Les Fêtes du mariage de Ferdinand de Médicis et de Christine de Lorraine, I: Musique des intermèdes de 'La Pellegrina'*, ed. D. P. Walker, Federico Ghisi, and Jean Jacquot (Paris, 1963), pp. 2–8 and 98–106.

[2] On monophonic ricercari in general, and especially those by Aurelio Virgiliano, see Imogene Horsley, 'The Solo Ricercar in Diminution Manuals: New Light on Early Wind and String Technique', *Acta musicologica* 33 (1961): 29–39. For a large mid-seventeenth-century collection of monophonic compositions for the recorder, see Jacob van Eyck, *Der Fluyten Lust-hof*, ed. Gerritt Vellekoop, 3 vols. (Amsterdam, 1957-58).

down the entire range of whatever instrument the student plays. Presumably the exercises not only prepare the student's fingers to cope with real diminutions but also his musical imagination, by fixing in his mind through constant repetition a store of stereotyped figuration patterns. I need hardly point out that this method of teaching by sequential repetition, first introduced by Rogniono in 1592, is still the way performers today learn the basic techniques of their instruments.

Conforto, who is, along with Maffei and Bovicelli, one of the chief sources of information about specifically vocal ornamentation in the late sixteenth century, published his systematic tables of *passaggi* in slightly more condensed form than other authors. He not only indicates that all his examples can be played in any one of seven clefs to fit voices or instruments of every range — various other authors do the same — but also includes a choice of two or three alternative notes or groups of notes in every diminution pattern, so that each single example can be resolved in several different ways (see Example 12).[1] Conforto's book was clearly designed for beginners: he promises anyone who is content to ornament only with semiquavers (*crome*) that he can memorize enough patterns in nine days, one day each for ascending and descending seconds, thirds, fourths, fifths, and one for unisons, so that they will be able to improvise in less than twenty days. For those who understand counterpoint he briefly remarks on the importance of considering the intervallic relationship between the bass and the note to be ornamented, but in order to help those who know no music theory, he marks with an x three diminutions, one moving chiefly in semiminims, one in *crome*, and one in *semicrome*, for each basic interval that will not produce untoward dissonances whether the bass is an octave, a tenth, or a twelfth below the main note.[2] In short, Conforto takes some care to explain exactly how his book may be used even by people who are musically inexperienced. Thus, even though every teacher of ornamentation arranges his material in a conventional way, differences among them do emerge. Ganassi emphasizes irregular rhythmic groupings, Ortiz stresses simple *passaggi* and cadential

[1] Conforto, *Breve et facile maniera*, p. 3.

[2] *Ibid.*, pp. 37–38, and, in German, pp. *15–16.

formulas, Dalla Casa seems preoccupied with speed, Rogniono with finger exercises, and Conforto with efficiency and the beginner.

Moreover, to say that *passaggi* are stereotyped melodic formulas is somewhat misleading, for the authors of the various instruction books seldom copy each other's formulas exactly. Even though the technique of

Example 12   Conforto's ornaments

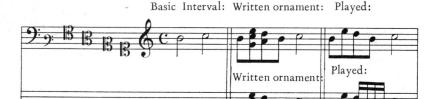

ornamenting remained the same during the entire century, the style of the embellishments did change from writer to writer and from generation to generation. Ortiz's ornaments, for example, are very different from Bovicelli's, even though both musicians went about adding them in exactly the same way. As Zacconi says, 'gl'acuti ingegni' are always inventing new embellishments to replace those that have become out of date.[1] To a certain extent these differences are an inevitable result of the technique employed. That is, if a musician divides an interval into three or four notes of smaller value while preserving the original harmonic implications and

[1] Zacconi, bk. I, chap. 66, fol. 58, and, in German, in Chrysander, p. 341.

staying within the stylistic framework of sixteenth-century music, his choice is extremely limited, and most manuals of ornamentation do in fact contain the same sorts of very simple embellishments.[1] But, as we have seen, sixteenth-century musicians more often divide an interval into ten, twelve, or even more smaller notes, and then the choice is so wide that two writers can hardly be expected ever to agree.

[1] Compare, for example, Ganassi, English and German translations, p. 32; Ortiz, p. 48; and Maffei's diminutions in Bridgman, 'Maffei et sa lettre sur le chant', p. 20.

3

COMPOSITIONS ORNAMENTED BY SIXTEENTH-CENTURY MUSICIANS

The best way to form an impression of the musical personalities of each of the teachers of ornamentation is to examine their embellishments of actual compositions. Most of the volumes include, after the systematic tables of *passaggi*, a collection of decorated voice parts, taken largely from motets and madrigals, and these, along with the anthologies of lute and keyboard music, comprise our principal source of information about how virtuosi actually performed during the Renaissance. Or at the very least the examples show us what teachers of ornamentation, if not virtuosi, considered to be suitable embellishments, and thus give us some notion of how tastes changed during the century.

The two rather artlessly decorated chansons and one Latin canon in Coclico's *Compendium* of 1552 are the earliest examples in the theoretical literature of complete compositions provided with written-out embellishments.[1] Coclico provides both superius and bass parts of the chansons with almost constant *passaggi*, even though that procedure contradicts his statement that the bass should not be decorated since it is the fundamental voice. His ornaments move chiefly in semiminims (quavers in the musical examples) with some *crome* (semiquavers), and he tends to use the same

figures more than once: he is fond of the rhythm ♩ ♪ ♪ ♪ ♫ , for

example, and when 'Languir me fault' repeats its opening phrase he simply

---

[1] Coclico, fols. I1ᵛ–3ᵛ, publishes an embellished canon with the text, 'Tendit ad artua virtus', as well as decorated versions of 'Languir me fault' and 'C'est a grand tort', which are based on slightly different chansons from those by Claudin de Sermisy, most easily accessible in a modern edition in Albert Seay, ed., *Pierre Attaingnant: Transcriptions of Chansons for Keyboard* (American Institute of Musicology, 1961), pp. 103–4 and 114–15. The written-out embellishments for vocal ensemble by Finck and Maffei are discussed below.

marks the repetition rather than devising new diminutions. Like Coclico's three pieces, the one complete composition embellished for solo performance in Maffei's letter on ornamentation (1562), the superius part of a madrigal by Francesco Layolle in four sections, 'Vago augelletto', uses a restricted number of melodic formulas.[1] Maffei prefers simple turn-like figures when decorating stepwise progressions (Example 13). A large percentage

Example 13 Maffei's ornamentation of 'Vago augelletto'

of. his *passaggi* consists of these simple patterns, which move twice as fast as Coclico's, in *crome* rather than semiminims, and alternate with the unadorned notes of the original rather than replacing them completely.

[1] Modern edition in Bridgman, pp. 31–33.

While Coclico and Maffei offer isolated examples of diminutions applied to the musical repertoire, Diego Ortiz furnishes an extensive collection of them in his treatise on viol playing of 1553, the only such collection before the several large ornamentation books of the 1580s and 1590s, and in many ways the most satisfactory of all artistically. Along with newly invented florid contrapuntal lines to be played over a cantus firmus, 'La Spagna', originally a *basse dance* melody, or against a predetermined series of chords, the so-called Italian tenors,[1] Ortiz also includes elaborated versions of a madrigal and a chanson, Jacques Arcadelt's 'O felici occhi miei' and Pierre Sandrin's 'Doulce memoire'.[2] Ortiz writes that viol players may wish to perform these compositions by repeating them two or three times, each time with newly varied decorations.[3] In order to show how such variation sets can be improvised, Ortiz presents each composition in four versions, with the bass embellished, with the superius embellished, with a technically more difficult bass part, less closely related to the vocal original than the first, and, finally with an independent, newly composed fifth voice, for bass viol, added to the original four. Like Maffei, Ortiz alternates unadorned notes with *passaggi* — perhaps slightly more than half of the original notes are embellished. The result is an evenly flowing melodic variation, with no abrupt changes of pace. While the original moves mostly in minims and crotchets (semibreves and minims in the original notation), the Ortiz variations proceed mainly in crotchets and semiquavers (minims and *crome* in the original), consistently faster than the vocal model. Like both Coclico and Maffei, Ortiz restricts the number of formulas he uses in any one version, but Ortiz carries this tendency further and often repeats the same motive two or three times in various transpositions[4] (Example 14) before dropping it in favour of a new one, similarly treated. In other words, Ortiz adds a new dimension of motivic interplay to each of his arrangements, a thematic

---

[1] The *recercadas* over Italian tenors are discussed in Gustave Reese, 'The Repertoire of Book II of Ortiz's *Tratado*', in *The Commonwealth of Music*, ed. Gustave Reese and Rose Brandel (New York, 1965), pp. 201–7. Further information about the contents of the Ortiz volume may be found in Brown, *Instrumental Music*, under 1553$_5$ and 1553$_6$.

[2] Ortiz, pp. 69–85 and 86–106.

[3] *Ibid.*, p. 68, and, in German, p. xxxvi.

[4] E.g., *ibid.*, pp. 79–80.

element totally absent from the vocal model. Indeed, a significant part of the charm of these arrangements consists of the surprise in finding consistent figuration patterns applied to passages where one would least expect them. Conversely, repetitions in the vocal model almost always call forth

Example 14
Ortiz. Third recercada on Arcadelt, 'O felici occhi miei', excerpt,

new embellishments from Ortiz, this process of constant renewal of the decorations being the standard practice of the century. Apparently musicians took pleasure in obscuring the structural elements of a composition, rather than in making them as plain as possible. Ortiz's diminutions on the superius of Arcadelt's 'O felici occhi miei'[1] (example 5B) may be considered a typical example of his style of ornamentation, even though here

1 *Ibid.*, pp. 76-78.

the literal repetition of motives is less evident than a tendency to repeat

the same rhythmic figure, ♩. ♪ ♪ ♪ ♪ ♪ , one of his favourite

patterns. As in most of his variations, the melodic outline of the original is still just discernible under the even application of semiquaver *passaggi*.

In spite of their differences, Coclico, Maffei, and Ortiz all wrote *passaggi* in approximately the same style, and their similarities to one another are especially obvious when their work is compared with the treatises from the last twenty years of the sixteenth century. These three musicians, then, probably preserve the central tradition of improvised ornamentation during the first three quarters of the century. Even though Coclico's embellishments move more slowly than the others, and Ortiz's are more skilfully arranged, all three musicians apply their *passaggi* evenly, speeding up the original melodic line but without causing any abrupt rhythmic shifts. The practitioners of the new style of the 1580s and 1590s, on the other hand, pile onto comparatively simple melodic lines excessively florid ornaments of awesome speed, while at the same time leaving more of the original notes unadorned than the earlier musicians did, so that the newer music is characterized by rapid changes of pace from slow to very fast indeed.

Girolamo dalla Casa, whose treatise of 1584 first announced the new style, writes diminutions that are typical of almost all of these late sixteenth-century decadent virtuosi. His treatise is divided into two books.[1] In the first, after the traditional systematic tables, he embellishes selected excerpts from the superius parts of various secular compositions, mostly madrigals by Rore, Striggio, and others, but including a few chansons as well. These passages and cadences, 'passi et cadenze' as he calls them, are arranged according to the speed of the decoration, first semiquavers alone, then demisemiquavers alone, then semiquavers and demisemiquavers combined, and so on, until he has introduced demisemiquaver triplets as well as hemi-demisemiquavers. At the end of this first book, parts of six compositions are fitted out with ornaments using all four of the time values that are

[1] The contents of both books are listed in Brown, as 1584₁ and 1584₂.

necessary, according to Dalla Casa, for the true art of embellishment. He decorates excerpts rather than complete superius parts because he apparently intended his diminutions to be incorporated into ensemble rather than solo performances;[1] since some opportunities had to be left for the other performers to ornament their own parts, he was content to apply diminutions to five or six passages only of the superius. For example, Dalla Casa chose the five excerpts from the superius of Alessandro Striggio's 'Anchor ch'io possa dire' which are bracketed in Example 15[2] to decorate with the diminutions shown in Example 16.[3] Even a glance at these *passaggi* suffices for one to grasp the novelty of the style. Instead of constituting a motivic superstructure or a uniformly paced melodic variation, Dalla Casa's *passaggi* are sporadic and rhapsodic bursts of small notes, too fast for the sort of rhythmic differentiation found in the earlier examples, let alone for the establishment of clearly profiled motives. Moreover when the *passaggi* of Example 16 are performed as intended, replacing the bracketed sections of Example 15, the rhythm alternates abruptly between the slower motion of the unadorned original and the frenzied pace of the embellishments. Clearly Dalla Casa's chief goal was not the invention of a sophisticated variation but rather the more primitive desire to show off his manual dexterity; he asks merely that the listener marvel at the agile throat or fingers of the performer.

In his second book, Dalla Casa furnishes embellishments for a series of complete voice parts, presumably to be performed as solos with the remaining voices played on lute or keyboard. First of all, there are nine superius parts of chansons arranged for a solo instrument. In these, as in the excerpts given in his first book, Dalla Casa leaves more of the notes undecorated than earlier musicians did, but makes up for this restraint by the flamboyance of those embellishments he does add. The first several phrases of Clemens non Papa's 'Frisque et gaillard' (Example 17) are

---

[1] As is evident from the fact that he writes (bk. I, fol. A2) that 'questi Madrigali li potrete sonar in compagnia'.

[2] Alessandro Striggio, *Il primo libro delli Madrigali a sei voci* (Venice: Girolamo Scotto, 1566), no. 3.

[3] Dalla Casa, bk. I, p. 39. I have omitted from Example 16e a second decorated version of the same passage, to be used when it returns at the end of the madrigal.

Example 15   Striggio's 'Anchor ch'io possa dire' (superius)

An - - chor ch'io pos-sa di - - re   che
(a)

d'ha-ver vi - ta il cor sol   tan - to   sen -   te

Quant' a voi son pre - sen - te,   quant' a voi son pre-sen-
(b)

- te,   Poi   che non m'e con-ces -

-so   Es - - ser vi ogn'hor ap -pres-so   Mai

non vor-rei ve -ni - re   Mai non vor-rei ve - ni - - re
(c)   (d)

Mia vi-ta in -nan - zi a voi ___   Tant'ho do-lor, tant'

ho do - lor   de la par-ti - - ta po- -i,   de

(e)

la par-ti-ta po - i,   de la par-ti - ta   po - - i

Example 16
Dalla Casa's ornaments for Striggio's 'Anchor ch'io possa dire'

(a)

(b)

typical.[1] Dalla Casa does follow earlier practice in devising new ornamentation whenever melodic material repeats, confirming once again the impression that performers in the sixteenth century were more concerned to obscure than to reveal the structural features of a composition. After these instrumental versions of superius parts, Dalla Casa next presents ten chansons and madrigals arranged specifically for viola bastarda, the small bass viola da gamba, called lyra viol in English, for which a special playing technique developed during the sixteenth century.[2] Its small size facilitated fast passage work and wide leaps, and Dalla Casa, as well as Rogniono in 1592, wrote out special diminutions for the instrument that took advantage of its capabilities.[3] Like a few of the Ortiz variations for bass viol, those by Dalla Casa for viola bastarda embellished mainly the bass line with many more leaps than usual, but they also skip from time to time up to one of the upper voices, so that the part, a composite of several lines of the original, covers a far wider range than normal. The opening phrases of Rore's 'Anchor che co'l partire'[4] (Example 18), as arranged by Dalla Casa for viola bastarda, demonstrate this technique very well. After these examples, idiomatically conceived for a specific instrument, Dalla Casa continues with five embellished madrigals supplied with text and intended for vocal performance. They are 'madrigali da cantar in compagnia, e anco co'l liuto solo', that is, superius parts that can be sung either as part of an ensemble or as solo songs to the lute.[5] While possibly a bit more restrained than the instrumental arrangements, these vocal embellishments nevertheless demonstrate the same stylistic traits as the others in the volume. Dalla Casa's variation on the superius of 'Anchor che co'l partire'[6]

[1] Dalla Casa, bk. II, p. 5, as 'Frais & gaillart'. The vocal model is published in Jacobus Clemens non Papa, *Opera Omnia*, ed. K. Ph. Bernet Kempers (American Institute of Musicology, 1962) 10: 17.

[2] On the viola bastarda or lyra viol, see Dalla Casa, bk. II, fol. 1ᵛ, and Sybil Marcuse, *Musical Instruments: A Comprehensive Dictionary* (New York, 1964), pp. 320–31 and 566. On the extensive English repertoire of the lyra viol, see Nathalie Dolmetsch, *The Viola da Gamba* (New York, 1926), pp. 74–77, and the bibliography of printed music for the lyra viol by Frank Traficante in *The Lute Society Journal* 8 (1966): 7–24.

[3] For some examples of embellished lines for the lyra viol, see Ferand, *Die Improvisation in Beispielen*, pp. 38–51 and 63–74.

[4] Dalla Casa, bk. II, p. 20.

[5] As Dalla Casa writes, *ibid.*, bk. II, p. 30.

[6] *Ibid.*, bk. II, p. 35. The unadorned superius is taken from Gertrude Parker Smith, ed., *The Madrigals of Cipriano de Rore for 3 and 4 Voices* (Northampton, Mass., 1943), pp. 45–47.

Example 17

Dalla Casa's ornaments for Clemens non Papa's 'Frisque et gaillard'

Example 18
Dalla Casa's version of Rore's 'Anchor che co'l partire' for viola bastarda

(Example 19b), for instance, ornaments fewer notes than a similar arrangement by Ortiz would, but it does erupt from time to time with showers of small notes. The second book of Dalla Casa's treatise closes with a single madrigal to which Dalla Casa has added embellishments in all four voices.[1]

---

[1] Dalla Casa, bk. II, pp. 38–49. One section of the madrigal is published in modern edition in Ferand, *Die Improvisation in Beispielen*, pp. 57–62.

Example 19   Rore 'Anchor che co'l partire'
The original version

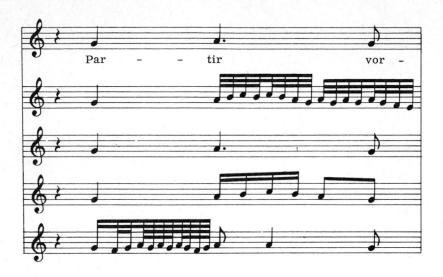

Giovanni Bassano, in his collection of madrigals, motets, and chansons published in 1591, follows Dalla Casa's lead in piling on excessively florid *passaggi*, but only sporadically. Bassano includes ornamented bass parts, superius parts, and composite lines derived from more than one voice of the model, as well as compositions with both bass and superius decorated. He says that his examples can be performed by voices or instruments, or 'in concerto' with his embellished line sung and the other parts taken by an instrumental ensemble or by a single keyboard instrument with the bass line doubled in proto-Baroque basso continuo scoring — indeed, he says that the bass ought always to be doubled since it is the fundamental voice.[1] He includes three versions of Rore's 'Anchor che co'l partire', one of which is a composite of more than one line and hence probably designed for the viola bastarda,[2] and two embellished versions of the superius.[3] The simpler of the two decorated superius parts consists largely of written-out graces of various sorts with occasional florid running passages, while the second of the two (Example 19c) includes some graces but concentrates on figuration patterns, including some (e.g., in bars 5–6) which have sharply profiled motives unusual for this late style. In this variation, as in many of the others, the fastest, longest, and most elaborate decoration is saved for the final cadence.

The remaining two late sixteenth-century teachers of ornamentation, Rogniono and Bovicelli, differ from Dalla Casa and Bassano in that they revert to the earlier practice of applying ornamentation to almost every note. But their *passaggi* still shift abruptly from slow to fast notes, because some of their decorations merely fill in leaps by passing notes, or else comprise adjacent notes, anticipations, portamenti, or other simple embellishments, while extremely rapid *passaggi* still disrupt the prevailing moderate pace from time to time. Rogniono includes in his treatise two versions of the superius of 'Anchor che co'l partire',[4] the range of which, by the way, suggests that they might have been primarily intended for the cornetto, as well as two composite lines for the viola bastarda.[5] He is far

[1] Bassano, *Motetti, madrigali et canzoni francese* (manuscript copy of 1591 ed.), p. 5.
[2] *Ibid.*, no. 20, p. 28.
[3] *Ibid.*, no. 4, p. 10, and no. 19, p. 27.
[4] Rogniono, *Passaggi*, bk. II, fols. H2 and H3.
[5] *Ibid.*, fols. H4 and H4ᵛ.

and away the most flamboyant exhibitionist of the group. The more difficult of his two superius parts (Example 19d), for instance, exemplifies the most extreme sort of virtuoso egomania to be found in the sixteenth century, and the composer's original intentions are completely obscured under the onslaught of Rogniono's incessant running figures, turns, and trills. Bovicelli, on the other hand, writes embellishments that are more idiomatically conceived for the human voice than anyone else's. He envelops the original vocal line with the sorts of graces that are more often associated with seventeenth-century music — slides up a third to the main note, intervals of a third filled in by step with an anticipation added, embellished anticipations, lower appoggiaturas, single mordents, inverted mordents, and various kinds of turns — which are interrupted once or twice in each phrase by fast running passages, that is, by the *passaggi* proper.[1]

In short, Dalla Casa's abrupt flights of fancy, Bassano's written-out graces, Rogniono's excesses, and Bovicelli's vocalisms are all varieties of the same florid style of embellishment that predominated during the 1580s and 1590s. But while it is true that the tastes of the time apparently approved of ever more and faster ornamentation, one should guard against the over-simple view that the history of improvised embellishment in the sixteenth century is a steady progression from simple to more complex, for whenever the unique qualities of individuals are valued — and the sixteenth century is the first golden age of the virtuoso performer — historical trends are counterbalanced by the idiosyncrasies of single artists. Thus it would seem that there were in the sixteenth century as many different styles of embellishment as there were virtuosi, and, indeed, a number of writers make the point that ornamentation ought to become a part of the performer's personal style. The sensitive musician, then, will cultivate a repertoire of *passaggi* that emphasizes his natural gifts. Hermann Finck, for example, writes that the practice of ornamentation depends on the agility, the aptitude, and the temperament of the individual performer,[2] and Ortiz says as much when he states that the effectiveness of *passaggi*

---

[1] His two versions of Rore's 'Anchor che co'l partire' are to be found in Bovicelli, *Regole*, pp. 46–49 and 50–53. The beginning of the first version is shown in example 19e. The second version is a sacred contrafactum set to a text beginning 'Angelus ad Pastores ait'.

[2] See Schlecht, p. 139.

depends on the ability of the player to perform them well.[1] So the manuals of ornamentation, while enabling the unimaginative to add melodic clichés mechanically to any composition, also free the more gifted to express their own personalities within the stylistic conventions of the time, albeit often at the expense of what many people then, as now, considered the performer's most serious mission, fulfilling as well as possible the composer's original intention.

In spite of the tendency of late sixteenth-century musicians to bury compositions under an avalanche of excessive decoration, then, some performers may have exercised more restraint. Certainly the tenor part of the motet, 'Quae est ista', as embellished by Zacconi in 1592,[2] more closely resembles the simpler style prevalent during the earlier parts of the century. And, conversely, some earlier musicians may have preferred diminutions that were more ornate than the usual ones. For example, *passaggi* approaching the complexity of those by late sixteenth-century musicians can be devised using only the tables published by Ganassi in 1535.

It is unfortunate that Ganassi, unlike most of the other teachers of ornamentation, did not include in his book any examples of complete compositions embellished, since *Fontegara* is the earliest of the diminution manuals and the only one published during the first half of the sixteenth century. Nevertheless some impression of the effects he wished can be gained by actually decorating a composition of the sort he might have played with *passaggi* taken exclusively from his tables. In writing these ornaments down, by the way, I am following the advice of at least one sixteenth-century musician, Diego Ortiz,[3] for what is lost in spontaneity is certainly more than regained in organization and security. And this exercise in 'applied musicology' offers an opportunity to explore questions of immediate importance to anyone involved in the problems of reconstructing earlier performing conventions. The superius of Jacques Arcadelt's madrigal, 'O felici occhi miei' (Example 5a), already used to demonstrate graces as well

---

[1] Ortiz, p. 5, and, in German, p. xxix.
[2] Zacconi, bk. I, chap. 66, fols. 63ᵛ–64ᵛ, and, in German, in Chrysander, pp. 365–68.
[3] Ortiz, p. 7, and, in German, p. xxxi.

as the ornamenting styles of Ortiz,[1] furnishes a convenient vehicle for embellishing in the manner of Ganassi (Example 5c).

Lest there be any doubt about how to appliqué the *passaggi* provided in the systematic tables onto a melodic line, I have bracketed each basic interval of the first few bars of the original. More often than not, the basic interval has been calculated as the distance from the beginning of one minim (semibreve in the original notation) to the beginning of the next, ignoring the intervening notes as Ganassi implies, so that his ornaments can be transferred without change from his tables to the madrigal superius. But occasionally, as in bars 14–15, the distance between two crotchets (minims in the original) has been considered the basic shape, and Ganassi's *passaggi* have then been halved in value.

For each interval Ganassi offers five to ten alternatives. Even after those *passaggi* that will produce impossible dissonances with the other voices have been eliminated, as well as those *passaggi* that go beyond the range of the singer or of the player's instrument, some choice among the remaining ornaments still remains, and it is here that a performer's taste can transform a mechanical exercise into an art. Good taste may be an unfortunate virtue to bring up in connection with the process of elaborately embellishing an already carefully written composition, for the demands of virtuosity are not always consonant with qualities of restraint, balance, and proportion. And yet taste is a topic that many of the teachers of ornamentation do discuss, even though their examples sometimes belie their words. Some of them warn performers not to attempt ornaments they cannot control perfectly and point out that a few ornaments played well are greatly to be preferred to many played badly.[2] Rogniono thinks that instrumentalists are more prone to excess than singers, and recommends his own finger exercises as a curb on sloppy extravagance.[3] As usual, however, it is Zacconi who gives the best and most detailed advice.[4] Indeed, in this respect his judgment is harsher than anyone else's, for he says flatly

---

[1] See n. 3, p. 49.

[2] See, for example, Ortiz, p. 5, and, in German, p. xxix; and Finck as quoted in Schlecht, p. 138. Dalla Casa, bk. I, fol. A2ᵛ, gives the most succinct advice: 'Poi nella Minuta far poca robba, ma buona'.

[3] Rogniono, bk. I, fol. A2ᵛ.

[4] Zacconi, bk. I, chap. 66, fols. 58ᵛ and 64ᵛ, and, in German, in Chrysander, pp. 343, and 368.

that musicians who cannot perform *passaggi* well ought to leave them out entirely. A singer who is adept at adding the few simple ornaments which suffice for most occasions should be satisfied with his ability. Florid ornamentation is pleasing to the ears, Zacconi writes, but he has found that composers sometimes avoid having their music performed rather than giving it to a singer known for his extravagance, for they prefer to hear what they themselves have written.

Nevertheless, Zacconi offers some sensible practical suggestions for controlling the impulse to embellish immoderately.[1] He recommends, for example, that the singer always try out a new diminution figure in ensembles rather than in a solo, for its faults will be less conspicuous that way, and he can benefit from the advice of his colleagues. Moreover, no one should ever sing more *passaggi* than he can manage in one breath. And singers should use, wherever they can, the same melodic formulas in different ways, for 'embellishment consists not so much in the variety or diversity of the *passaggi* as in a moderate and limited number of figures.'[2] Zacconi implies, then, not only that each musician ought to perfect a relatively restricted number of *passaggi* that he is expert at using, but also that the same figure may recur from time to time throughout a piece, transposed, slightly changed, or in a new musical context, a point that Bovicelli also makes.[3] In other words, Zacconi encourages the performer to add to a composition in his improvisation a new element of motivic interplay, quite independent of the composer's intention, just as Ortiz was wont to do. I have taken his advice only once in the written-out embellishment of 'O felici occhi miei', in bars 26–28, the only passage which departs in any way from Ganassi's tables. But if my version is to be condemned as excessive, and my own example thus to belie my words, I would plead that it is precisely the diversity of Ganassi's *passaggi*, and especially his rhythmic irregularities, that I wished to demonstrate. A more tasteful arrangement would doubtless follow Zacconi's recommendations more closely in restricting the number and the variety of the figuration patterns.

[1] Zacconi, fols. 59 and 62ᵛ, and, in German, in Chrysander, pp. 345–46 and 360.
[2] Zacconi, fol. 75ᵛ, '... la gorgia non tanto consiste nella variatione, ò nella diversità de passaggi, quanto che in una giusta, et terminata quantità di figure...' and, in German, in Chrysander, p. 394.
[3] Bovicelli, p. 10.

4

SOLO AND ENSEMBLE

Any value judgment about the amount of ornamentation that ought to be considered excessive has to take the number of performers into account. Embellishments intended for an ensemble of singers or instrumentalists should be fewer and simpler than those improvised by a single lutenist or keyboard player, or by a solo singer, or recorder or viol player. The canon of taste in the sixteenth century permitted a soloist greater freedom than an ensemble performer. Thus my version of 'O felici occhi miei' in the manner of Ganassi might not have been considered too elaborate if performed by a single singer or recorder player with Arcadelt's lower voices played on a lute or keyboard, but it certainly contains too many embellishments for a performance by four singers or players. This distinction between solo and ensemble improvisation is clearly made in the theoretical literature, most of which is primarily intended for soloists. Ganassi, for example, explicitly states that his advice is to apply only to solo playing, but he fails to note how ensemble playing differs save in the obvious respect that every musician must try to match his fellow players.[1] Ortiz clarifies somewhat the differences between the two sorts of improvisation in dividing his treatise into two books, the first of which is for ensemble players and consists of systematic tables of ornaments, while the second contains actual examples of embellished compositions arranged for solo performance.[2] This division explains why Ortiz's tables are simpler than those by other authors, and why Ortiz emphasizes cadential formulas: ensemble embellishments ought not to be elaborate, and they are largely restricted to cadences.

[1] Ganassi, *Fontegara*, chap. 25.
[2] As he explains, *Tratado*, p. 5, and, in German, p. xxix.

But it is Giovanni Camillo Maffei who gives the most detailed advice about ensemble improvisation in his letter on embellishments written in 1562.[1] After supplying his readers with an example, a Layolle madrigal to which some *passaggi* have been added in all voices, Maffei formulates five rules for ensemble singing which seem sensible enough to serve as a guide for ornamenting any polyphonic music of the century, even though they need not be followed slavishly. His first rule confirms the implied practice of Ortiz and others in stating that ornaments are to be added primarily at cadences, and it is followed quite literally in Maffei's example. Especially when the voices cadence at different times, each can add ornaments without getting in the way of the others. Maffei also allows some embellishments within a phrase, but his second rule cautions singers not to add ornaments to more than four or five passages in any one composition, lest the listener be satiated, as he says so often happens. He evidently means that each singer can improvise four or five *passaggi* per composition, for he himself uses approximately that number in each of the four voices of the Layolle madrigal. His next two rules are intended specifically for singers and refer to the handling of the text. The first recommends that *passaggi* be applied only to the penultimate syllables of words so that the end of the ornament will coincide with the end of the word. Maffei himself does not always follow this rule — he sometimes decorates monosyllabic words, for example — but even in his exceptions he never violates what is the implicit assumption of the rule, namely, that *passaggi* should fall on long and never on short syllables. Moreover, singers should take care to embellish only those vowels that are convenient for melismas. *O* is the best vowel and *i* and *u* are the two worst, for a diminution sung on the former sounds like a lost baby animal crying for its mother, while one sung on the latter resembles the howling of a wolf. Maffei's fifth and last rule for group embellishment advises each singer in a group of four or five to be careful to give way to the others so that two singers do not ornament simultaneously, a circumstance that merely serves to confound the harmony.

[1] The five rules, along with the Layolle madrigal, are printed in Bridgman, pp. 28–29 and 22–27. The madrigal is also published in a modern edition in Ferand, *Die Improvisation in Beispielen*, pp. 52–56 and 165.

Two sixteenth-century musicians besides Maffei have left us written-out examples of ensemble improvisation. Hermann Finck includes an embellished motet in his treatise,[1] and Dalla Casa, as we have seen, not only ornaments excerpts from superius parts that are meant to be incorporated into ensemble performances but also prints in his treatise one complete madrigal, Rore's setting of the Petrarch sestina, 'Alla dolc'ombra', with *passaggi* supplied for all four voices.[2] In addition, Dalla Casa published in 1591 a whole volume of his own madrigals, unfortunately incompletely preserved, to which he likewise added embellishments in all voices.[3] Quite naturally, Maffei obeyed his own rules more or less closely in ornamenting the Layolle madrigal. To a surprising extent Finck and Dalla Casa confirm the general validity of Maffei's remarks in following the same procedures. True, they consistently ignore Maffei's prohibition against singing melismas on *i* and *u*, and they both embellish more, but not many more, than four or five passages in each voice. They do, however, concentrate their decorations at cadences and on penultimate syllables, and they do avoid simultaneous *passaggi*. Maffei applied ornaments more or less evenly to all of the voices. Finck favours the top voice somewhat, and Dalla Casa goes even further in the same direction. Dalla Casa says, in the preface to his second book, that the superius is often supplied with the most *passaggi*, and he proceeds to do just that.[4] Apparently sixteenth-century musicians did not agree entirely about the virtue of an even application of ornamentation. Finck, even though he is slightly more generous in giving *passaggi* to the superius, advocates having all voices share in the embellishment, but he mentions musicians who prefer to reserve ornaments only for the bass or the superius.[5] Zacconi prints some ornaments, simpler than most, specifically for basses when they function as supports for higher voices.[6] And we have seen that Coclico expressly

---

[1] See Ferand, pp. 75–79, and Schlecht, pp. 156–64.

[2] See n. 1, p 42.

[3] Girolamo dalla Casa, *Il secondo libro de madrigali a cinque voci, con passaggi* . . . (Venice: Ricciardo Amadino, 1590). The tenor part book is missing from the unique set of parts in Vienna, Osterreichische Nationalbibliothek.

[4] *Il vero modo*, bk. II, fol. A1ᵛ.

[5] See Schlecht, p. 139.

[6] Bk. I, chap. 66, fol. 63, and, in German, in Chrysander, p. 363.

forbids decorating bass parts, even though he himself did so.[1] But in theory, at least, most musicians seem to favour allowing the bass, tenor, and alto parts as many, or almost as many, ornaments as the superius.

Sancta Maria writes that keyboard players ought not only to apply ornaments evenly, but also to make a point of adding the same embellishment each time a melody recurs, as for example in an imitative ricercar or canzona, even though such consistency is not always possible, either for musical or for physical reasons.[2] But such consistency is easier for a single keyboard player than for an ensemble of four, five, or more performers. Maffei, Finck, and Dalla Casa do sometimes repeat the same or similar *passaggi* in all parts in an imitative section, but more often they seem to prize independence and variety above uniformity — yet another indication that performers in the sixteenth century were relatively little concerned with making obvious the structural features of the music.

Hermann Finck reminds us that compositions sung by a chorus cannot be embellished, for with more than one singer on a part chaos would result if each of them improvised in his own way.[3] But even the simple and apparently obvious statement that ornaments may be added to a polyphonic composition only when the parts are sung or played by soloists, in order to avoid clashing simultaneous *passaggi*, must be hedged with some reservations, since a certain amount of heterophony was apparently tolerated and even encouraged in the sixteenth century. One kind of heterophony can be found in the Ortiz treatise. While he recommends that the keyboard player omit the superius part in his intabulation when it is the voice being decorated by the solo instrument, he does ask the accompanist in most of his variations to play the unadorned bass part at the same time that the solo viol embellishes it. A similar sort of heterophony, specifically linked with ensemble performance, is mentioned in Niccolò Vicentino's *Dialogo* of 1555.[4] Vicentino objects to the practice of impro-

---

[1] Fol. 13^v.

[2] Bk. I, chap. 23.

[3] See Schlecht, p. 140.

[4] Bk. IV, chap. 42, pp. 88 (recte 94)–95. See also G. Thibault, 'Du rôle de l'ornementation dans l'évolution de la musique', *International Musicological Society: Report of the Eighth Congress, New York, 1961* (Cassel, 1961) 1: 454, for an example of sixteenth-century heterophony involving instruments only.

vising diminutions in music for four voices, on the grounds that the ornaments depart from the written notes and thus leave the harmony bare. Singers should ornament, then, only music for five or more voices for the thicker texture ensures full harmonies even when *passaggi* are added. If singers insist on ornamenting music for four voices, Vicentino continues, they should take care always to have an instrumental ensemble double them, playing their parts exactly as written, and then the harmonies will be heard just as the composer intended them. A thorough study of the sixteenth-century practice of doubling singers with instruments needs to be made; it was almost certainly more common than is frequently supposed today.[1] For the present suffice it to say that Vicentino's statement shows that sixteenth-century musicians did tolerate the sort of heterophony that results when a singer embellishes a line that is being doubled by an instrumentalist playing the notes as written, and we shall presently see that the reverse was also practised, with the instrumentalist ornamenting while the singer stuck to the printed notes. Finck's warning against choral improvisation, on the other hand, makes clear that simultaneous embellishment by two singers sharing the same part was not permitted.

The practice of adding embellishments to cadences was widespread and unambiguous enough not to require further comment. A rule for deciding where else in a composition to add *passaggi* is not so easy to formulate. Diruta advises the keyboard player to apply *tremoli* at the beginning of ricercars and canzonas and whenever one hand is assigned a single line while the other plays chords,[2] but he is referring only to graces, used to emphasize single notes, rather than to *passaggi*, which tend to obscure the shape of a melodic line. Zacconi's discussion of the distribution of embellishments throughout a composition comes closer to describing the extant examples of ensemble improvisation, and so his remarks may well be taken as the most reliable guide to sixteenth-century common practice.[3]

[1] The best study of the subject thus far is Robert Weaver, 'Sixteenth-Century Instrumentation', *Musical Quarterly* 47 (1961): 363–78, but he emphasizes the symbolic use of instruments rather than practical problems of instrumentation. See also Howard Mayer Brown, 'Psyche's Lament: Some Music for the Medici Wedding in 1565', in *Words and Music: The Scholar's View. A Medley of Problems and Solutions Compiled in Honor of A. Tillman Merritt by Sundry Hands*, ed. Laurence Berman (Cambridge, Mass., 1971), and Brown, *Sixteenth-Century Instrumentation: The Music of the Florentine Intermedii*, Musicological Studies and Documents, vol. 30 (American Institute of Musicology, 1973).

[2] *Transilvano*, bk. I, p. 20, and, in German, in Krebs, p. 341.

[3] Bk. I, chap. 66, fol. 59, and, in German, in Chrysander, pp. 345–46.

In the first place, Zacconi advises against applying *passaggi* at the beginning of an imitative composition until after the second voice has entered, on the grounds that diminutions heard against slower-moving voices afford much more pleasure than those decorating a single unaccompanied line. He might well have said instead that the first several intervals of each phrase are the most important thematically, since they often comprise the most distinctive part of the melodic line, and imitation is frequently based exclusively on this opening motive. Thus embellishment should be delayed until enough of the melodic material has been stated to establish the identity of the phrase, as it were; and, by and large, the sixteenth-century musicians who have left us written-out improvisations follow this practice. Zacconi goes on to say that the simpler embellishments should appear at the beginning of a composition and that they should get more and more complex as the piece progresses, and he warns against saving all decoration until the very end, leaving the middle bare and empty. And this common-sense rule, to give shape to a composition by gradually increasing the density of ornamentation, has been put to practical use in many of the sixteenth-century embellished lines that have come down to us.

Zacconi's two basic rules for the distribution of embellishments — to delay their introduction until after the first few notes of a phrase are stated, and to arrange them in progressive order of complexity — were written for ensemble performers, but they apply as well to arrangements of polyphonic music for solo singer or instrumentalist with lute or keyboard accompaniment. Indeed, the chief difference between solo and ensemble improvisation seems to be merely the amount and complexity of the permissible decoration. Whereas each performer in an ensemble must be careful to allow opportunities for each of his colleagues to ornament in turn, the soloist is free to apply diminutions fairly evenly throughout a composition, striking his own balance between too much and too little. And ensemble performers are constrained to control the exuberance of their improvisation, whereas the extravagance of soloistic ornamentation was limited only by the single performer's imagination and his technical skill, if the surviving examples are to be believed. In short, ornamentation was applied to ensemble music as mere decoration — it was meant to enhance but not transform the original — while soloists improvised diminutions chiefly in order to display their virtuosity, even sometimes at the expense of the composer's intentions.

Simple decoration and virtuoso display are, then, the two primary functions of improvised ornamentation. But there is also a third kind: embellishment as acoustical reinforcement. Apparently some sixteenth-century musicians added diminutions to their parts in order to swell the total sound so that it better filled a large hall, when they doubled voices and other instruments in the large mixed ensembles that were characteristic of mid-sixteenth-century *intermedii*. The description of the music performed in the great hall of the Palazzo Vecchio in Florence as *intermedii*, when Francesco de' Medici married Joanna of Austria in 1565, furnishes information about this practice as well as other valuable details about the instrumentation and scoring of this sort of *intermedio* orchestra.[1] At the end of the first *intermedio* of the evening a madrigal was sung by five actor-singers on stage, accompanied back-stage by two harpsichords and bass lute, probably playing proto-continuo parts, four transverse flutes and one trombone, doubling the five singers, and a bass viol 'aggiunto sopra le parti', that is, added onto the other parts, as well as a descant viol and a recorder, similarly added. The second *intermedio* began with a madrigal sung by four actor-singers doubled by a mixed consort of viol, flute, recorder, and trombone, playing superius, altus, tenor, and bassus, as well as by four lutes, a second viol, a lira da gamba, three harpsichords plus bass lute, and a mute cornetto playing a fifth voice added to the soprano ('aggiunta di soprano'). The parts said to be added to both of these compositions can only have been lines embellished so elaborately that they sounded like new ones, or else genuinely new obbligati, improvised in the manner described by Diego Ortiz as one of the possible ways of arranging a composed piece for solo instrument and harpsichord.[2] In either case the effect of these fast-moving lines, contrasted with the slower, heavily doubled original ones, must have been to increase the density of sound, making as impressive a sonority as possible.

[1] O. G. Sonneck, 'A Description of Alessandro Striggio and Francesco Corteccia's Intermedi "Psyche and Amor", 1565', *Miscellaneous Studies in the History of Music* (New York, 1921; repr. ed., 1968), pp. 269–86, includes an English translation of the playwright Il Lasca's description of the *intermedii*. The original Italian is printed in Sonneck's article with the same title in *Musical Antiquary* 3 (1911): 40–53. The instruments for the first two *intermedii* are listed, *ibid.*, p. 52.

[2] Ortiz, p. 68, and, in German, p. xxxvi.

5

VOICES AND INSTRUMENTS

Whether ornaments were improvised by musicians playing in small or large ensembles, or by soloists, all authors agree that exactly the same technique was used, albeit applied in varying degrees of complexity, as we have seen. And the same kinds of ornaments were added by singers as by players of whatever instrument. It is, after all, a truism that music composed during the Renaissance did not take into account the idiomatic capabilities of specific instruments. Nevertheless, sixteenth-century musicians were certainly aware of the differences among their instruments and modified the basic technique of ornamentation in order to accommodate them. Both Rogniono and Zacconi, for example, point out that instruments are more adept at skips than singers and can improvise faster passage work, so that vocal ornamentation must necessarily be slower and largely restricted to stepwise motion.[1] Much of the text in Ganassi's *Fontegara* is taken up with explanations of quite subtle problems relating specifically to the manner of playing the recorder, and the same writer's *Regola Rubertina* explicitly discusses the way *passaggi* can best be adapted to the viol, by using higher left-hand positions to avoid having to change strings.[2] Dalla Casa praises the cornetto as the instrument most like the human voice and offers specific suggestions for playing embellishments on it.[3] And some differences between embellishments for lute and those for keyboard, caused by the physical restrictions imposed by the two kinds of instruments,

---

[1] Rogniono, bk. I, fol. A2ᵛ; and Zacconi, bk. I, chap. 66, fol. 60ᵛ, and, in German, in Chrysander, p. 354.

[2] Ganassi, *Fontegara*, chaps. 2–4, and *idem*, *Regola Rubertina, Lettione Secunda* (Venice, 1543), chaps, 17 and 18.

[3] Bk. I, fol. 2ᵛ.

can be noted in the musical literature.[1] In short, sixteenth-century discussions of ornamentation do recognize the nature and limitations of various instruments, especially those cultivated by amateurs for chamber music — the recorder, the viol, the lute, and keyboards[2] — even though idiomatic styles of embellishment were not developed for any one of them.

There are, however, several exceptions to this stylistic unity. As we have seen, musicians did develop a special kind of ornamentation for the viola bastarda, although it may be more accurate to say that the instrument was invented in order to accommodate the wide leaps, broken chords, and fast passage work that musicians wished to include in their improvisations. In any case its manner of playing, as its English name, lyra viol, attests, is almost certainly related to that of its cousin, the lira da braccio, the idiosyncrasies of which had long since been exploited by performers. While the history of the lira da braccio goes back at least to the early fifteenth century, the earliest reference to the pseudo-polyphonic technique of the viola bastarda occurs in 1539.[3] Another new instrument specifically designed to facilitate improvisation, the closely related lira da gamba or lirone, is mentioned for the first time in connection with the 1565 *intermedii*.[4] And in the 1590s the first idiomatically conceived orna-

---

[1] For a brief discussion of differences between lute and keyboard style in the sixteenth century, see Daniel Heartz, 'Les Styles instrumentaux dans la musique de la Renaissance', in *La Musique instrumentale de la Renaissance*, ed. Jean Jacquot (Paris, 1955), pp. 61–76.

[2] Those professional musicians who played shawms, cornetts, and trombones in ensembles of wind instruments almost certainly improvised the same sorts of embellishments as those added to chamber music. Ganassi and Dalla Casa, for example, were both members of such bands. But the embellishment manuals were not primarily intended for such professionals, who have, in fact, left us very little evidence of the details of their activities. See, for example, Polk, 'Flemish Wind Bands'.

[3] On the lira da braccio see n. 1, p. ix. On the viola bastarda see nn. 2 & 3, p. 40. Marcuse, *Musical Instruments*, pp. 320–31, states that the term 'viola bastarda' was used for the first time in 1589 (in the Florentine *intermedio* cited in n. 1, p. 27). But the madrigal by Francesco Corteccia, performed at a Florentine *intermedio* in 1539, by a singer 'con un violone sonando tutte le parti', described in Brown, *Instrumental Music*, as 1539₁, no. 13, and published in a modern edition in Arnold Schering, *Geschichte der Musik in Beispielen* (Leipzig, 1931), no. 99, uses exactly the same technique as the viola bastarda. Silvestro Ganassi, *Regola Rubertina*, *Lettione Secunda*, chap. 16, discusses the practice of playing multiple stops on the viol to accompany singing. Ganassi points out that chords are easier to play on the lute or lira da braccio than on the viol, so that the viol is really being used to imitate the lira.

[4] See Sonneck, pp. 52–53.

ment, the specifically vocal *trillo*, was introduced.[1] Little by little the single technique of embellishment disintegrated, as musicians gradually became interested in exploiting the unique qualities of the voice and of individual instruments. But this process of specialization, which forms an important chapter in the history of seventeenth-century music, had barely begun by the end of the sixteenth; the Renaissance gave way to the Baroque era in slow degrees.

On the other hand, one basic difference between vocal and instrumental ornamentation seems to have existed throughout the sixteenth century, if the tacit assumptions of the embellishment manuals can be accurately judged. Instrumentalists appear to regard improvised ornamentation as an integral part of their playing technique and instruction in the art of diminutions may have formed a part of the elementary training of almost everyone who learned an instrument. Thus, Ganassi says that three things are necessary to play the recorder — breath, fingers, and tongue — and that the effectiveness of the fingers depends on the ability to master various kinds of articulations and a knowledge of the art of playing divisions. The one skill, he says, is useless without the other.[2] Ortiz implies that embellishments are a necessary part of every instrumentalist's technical equipment when he says in his preface simply that he wishes to offer instruction in playing the viol;[3] in other words, he seems to be saying that his treatise supplies the information needed by every viol player, even though he discusses only improvisation. And similarly, the wording of Dalla Casa's preface of 1584 suggests that all instrumentalists but not all singers had to know how to play *passaggi*, for he says that his treatise is intended for all those who play instruments, but that he has included some examples for those singers who like to ornament, implying that not all did.[4]

Maffei writes in 1562 that the only way to give pleasure to the ear and sing in a courtly manner ('cantar cavaleresco') is by embellishing the parts,[5] but, as Bridgman points out,[6] in another letter he acknowledges

---

1 See n. 3, p. 10

2 Ganassi, *Fontegara*, chaps. 2 and 9.

3 Ortiz, p. 5, and, in German, p. xxix.

4 Bk. II, fol. A1ᵛ. Rogniono, bk. I, fol. A2ᵛ, also seems to suggest that instrumentalists were more familiar with techniques of embellishment when he says that they are more prone than singers to excess.

5 Bridgman, p. 33.

6 *Ibid.*, p. 9.

that not everyone could or would improvise *passaggi*, for he describes a gathering where no one agreed on how to perform the music, whether with or without instrumental doubling, improvised ornamentation, and so on. And we have already seen that sixteenth-century writers place some restrictions on vocal improvisations. Finck, for example, prohibits choral singers from adding *passaggi*, and he explains that some authorities permit only the bass or the superius parts to be decorated, although he recommends that all should.[1] Vicentino counsels against improvising ornaments in music for four or fewer voices.[2] And Conforto justifies writing his treatise on the grounds that vocal embellishments are commonly heard only in big cities and princely courts, and he would like to see the practice spread.[3] But once again it is Zacconi who presents the most comprehensive view of the situation.[4] Embellished song gives so much pleasure, he writes, that those who do not decorate their parts — there evidently were some, then — scarcely please their audiences and are not well thought of by other singers. Moreover, as we have seen, he counsels those who cannot perform *passaggi* perfectly not to attempt them at all. When we consider — he concludes his chapter on ornamentation — how difficult it is for the human voice to cope with so many fast notes, we ought also to think of those musicians with quite good voices, who can sing with security any music that is set before them, but who have no natural gift for diminutions. If they could take away this ability from those who possess it, they would; for singers with mediocre voices, who have mediocre careers, would live like *grands seigneurs* if they could improvise.

In short, the theoretical sources seem to indicate that only some singers but all instrumentalists had to be able to embellish their parts.[5] This conclusion is borne out, too, by the surviving musical literature. Intabulations for lute and keyboard of motets, madrigals, and chansons, almost all of them decorated, though in widely varying degrees, exist in plenty from

[1] Schlecht, pp. 139–40.
[2] Vicentino, p. 88 (*recte* 94).
[3] Conforto, pp. 33–34, and, in German, p.*10.
[4] Zacconi, fols. 58 and 77, and in German, in Chrysander, pp. 341–42 and 394–96.
[5] Present-day instrumentalists, therefore, viol and recorder players, especially those who wish to explore the possibilities of adapting the rich vocal literature of the sixteenth-century to their instruments, ought to feel more obliged than singers to add a moderate amount of ornamentation to all parts when they play in ensembles, using Maffei's rules as a guide.

every decade of the century. And the musical examples supplied by Ganassi, Ortiz, Dalla Casa, and Rogniono, while usable by singers, were primarily intended for instrumentalists; together these examples furnish a more or less comprehensive survey of instrumental practices from 1535 to the end of the century.[1] The first large collection of embellished vocal music, on the other hand, dates from 1590, the year Dalla Casa published his volume of *madrigali . . . con i passaggi*. Before that time the only compositions supplied with diminutions specifically intended for voices were the two short *giustiniani* in Petrucci's sixth book of *frottole* (1506),[2] the two short chansons and canon in Coclico's treatise of 1552, the single examples furnished by Finck (1556) and Maffei (1562), and the few vocal arrangements in Dalla Casa's instrumental treatise of 1584. If every singer, professional as well as amateur, had been expected to be able to embellish his part at sight as a matter of course, surely a more extensive body of theoretical literature and many more musical examples would have been required to supply singers with the skills they needed.

Since such material does not exist, it seems likely, then, that until late in the century only a portion of the total number of sixteenth-century singers cultivated the art of diminutions extensively. Perhaps all the better professionals did, especially those who considered themselves virtuosi. That conclusion would fit with Zacconi's remark that there were musically capable professionals who could not improvise even in 1592 when, clearly, the art was highly valued.[3] But Petrucci's *giustiniani* prove that the practice

[1] For a partial survey of Italian keyboard and lute music, see Howard Mayer Brown, 'Embellishment in Early Sixteenth-Century Italian Intabulations,' *Proceedings of the Royal Musical Association* 100 (1973–74).

[2] See Walter Rubsamen, 'The Justiniane or Viniziane of the 15th Century', *Acta musicologica* 29 (1957): 172–84. One of the compositions is published in a modern edition both in its unadorned and in its embellished state, there and in Ferand, *Die Improvisation in Beispielen*, pp. 30–32.

[3] Zacconi, fol. 71, and, in German, in Chrysander, pp. 394–95. The necessity for professional singers in the early seventeenth century to embellish well is shown by Claudio Monteverdi's evaluation of various singers whom he auditioned in Venice for positions with the Mantuan court. He invariably comments on their *trilli* and *gorgie* as well as their range, voice quality, and diction. See his letters in Gian Francesco Malipiero, *Claudio Monteverdi* (Milan, 1929), pp. 151 (no. 13), 237 (no. 78), 251 (no. 90), 259 (no. 94), 264 (no. 98), and 279 (no. 111). These letters are published in English translations in Denis Arnold and Nigel Fortune, 'The Man as seen through his Letters', in *The Monteverdi Companion*, ed. Arnold and Fortune (London, 1968), pp. 35 (no. 6), 60 (no. 21), 64 (no. 23), 69 (no. 27), 73 (no. 31), and 77 (no. 34).

was known as early as 1506, and, indeed, the extreme simplicity of the unadorned version of the same music in a fifteenth-century manuscript suggests that the practice was known much earlier. Petrucci also published schemata for singing any poem in various fixed forms, and their utter simplicity also strongly suggests embellished performance.[1] There are, in fact, a number of similar pieces of evidence that vocal improvisation occurred throughout the century. After all, the primarily instrumental embellishment manuals published from 1535 on all without exception explain that they can be used by singers.

The conclusion that sixteenth-century instrumentalists were more prone than singers to improvise ornaments, that, indeed, instrumental versions of vocal music may normally have been embellished and only exceptionally played as written, involves a paradox, for Ganassi, and later instrumentalists as well, insist on the inferiority of instruments to the human voice, and emphasize the fact that players should model themselves in every way, even including their style of ornamentation, on singers.[2] That advice reflects the fact that all instruments are in a sense merely mechanical extensions of the musician himself; and the model of a flexibly moulded, ideally contoured phrase is, even today, a so-called singing line, one, that is, which is played as nearly as possible as though produced by the human voice. But these sixteenth-century instrumentalists are also acknowledging the supremacy of vocal music before 1600; in saying that players ought to imitate singers they are thinking especially of one factor of performance that instrumentalists are apt to overlook, namely, the nature of the text and its meaning. Ganassi writes that the first care of a singer, when a piece of music is set before him, is to take into account the nature of the text.[3] If the words are happy, his performance will be lively, and if sad, he will sing softly and with melancholy. Vicentino is even more specific in stressing the dependence of a performance on the character of the text, for he maintains that both tempo and dynamics will change according to the

---

[1] See, for example, 'Modus dicendi Capitula' and 'Per sonetti', in Petrucci's frottola books I and III, published in Gaetano Cesari, Raffaele Monterosso, and Benvenuto Disertori, eds., *Le Frottole nell'edizione principe di Ottaviano Petrucci* (Cremona, 1954), pp. 36–37 and 127.

[2] See Ganassi, *Fontegara*, chaps. 1, 2, 13, 24, and 25; and Dalla Casa, bk. I, fol. 2[v].

[3] *Fontegara*, chap. 25.

passions of the words.[1] Both writers, and Bovicelli as well,[2] also point out that the number and kinds of improvised ornaments should also be controlled by the sense of the text. Lamentations and other sad pieces, for example, should never be embellished, according to Vicentino, though Bovicelli admits of some exception, and, conversely, happy texts can absorb the most *passaggi*.[3] Ideally, writes Ganassi,[4] the instrumentalist should express the meaning of the words so clearly that a listener can follow them even though they are totally absent.

Singers, of course, had an extra burden in improvising ornamentation, for they not only had to invent melodic figures extempore that fit the musical and poetic situation, but they also had to pronounce the words properly and adjust the text underlay to take the *passaggi* into account. All the authors who discuss vocal ornamentation remind their readers of the importance of good underlay and correct pronunciation, but only Bovicelli gives detailed rules for handling words disrupted by the addition of embellishments.[5] Most authors, however, in discussing the manner in which improvised ornaments ought to be performed, put most of their emphasis on two things: each note of the *passaggi* should be heard clearly and distinctly — no easy thing to do in view of their speed, especially for singers — and the tempo ought to be strictly maintained, without any slowing down to accommodate the greatly increased number of notes.[6] Bovicelli, it is true, makes one exception, and allows a ritardando at the final cadence,[7] since the penultimate note is apt to be decorated with the most complex embellishment of the entire composition. Rogniono even suggests keeping time with the foot, since the fingers and brain will

---

[1] Vicentino, pp. 88 (recte 94)–95.

[2] Bovicelli, p. 15.

[3] Exceptions to this rule can easily be found in the embellishment manuals as well as in the lute and keyboard repertoire. The first embellished superius in Bovicelli's own volume, for example, is a lover's lament, Palestrina's 'Io son ferito', and not all of the madrigals decorated by Dalla Casa have happy texts.

[4] *Fontegara*, chap. 1, where he likens the recorder player's dependence on singers to the painter's imitation of nature.

[5] They are readily accessible in the facsimile edition of Bovicelli, pp. 7–10.

[6] See Dalla Casa, bk. II, fol. 1ᵛ; Rogniono, bk. II, fol. C1ᵛ; Zacconi, fol. 58ᵛ, and, in German, in Chrysander, p. 344; and Bovicelli, p. 15.

[7] P. 15.

already be fully occupied.[1] The testimony of these sixteenth-century musicians should quell any suspicion that elaborately decorated arrangements of vocal music, including instrumental intabulations, might have been performed more slowly than the simple, original versions, in order to fit in all of the smallest notes. Indeed, discussions about the tempi proper for sixteenth-century music doubtless ought to take into consideration the possibilities of extravagant ornamentation, for surely an absolute limit to the speed at which hemidemisemiquavers can be played could easily be established.

Wind players who followed the advice of the teachers of ornamentation, and strove for accuracy and precision in playing *passaggi*, would have needed secure control over their tongues as well as their fingers. They would, in other words, have had to develop a kind of articulation suitable for fast passage work, and the embellishment manuals do in fact explain exactly how the tongue was to behave.[2] They all agree — although they do not all say so clearly and unambiguously — that all time values down to a semiquaver (*croma*) were normally tongued, either with a hard stroke, 'te te,' or a softer one, 'de de'.[3] For playing *passaggi*, musicians developed a series of faster articulations, so-called 'lingue rinverse', reversed tonguings or what we would call double tonguing, in which notes are attacked

---

[1] Bk. II, fol. C1ᵛ.

[2] Tonguing for wind players is discussed in Ganassi, *Fontegara*, chaps. 5–8; Martin Agricola, *Musica instrumentalis deudsch*, ed. Eitner, pp. 183–89; Dalla Casa, bk. I, fol. 2ᵛ; and Rogniono, bk. I, fol. A2ᵛ. Although they are not equally complete in their treatment of the subject, they all teach virtually the same tonguings, and seem to agree on general principles.

The only two modern discussions of sixteenth-century tonguings known to me are Imogene Horsley, 'Wind Techniques in the Sixteenth and Early Seventeenth Centuries', *Brass Quarterly* 4 (1960): 49–63, and George Houle, 'Tonguing and Rhythmic Patterns in Early Music', *American Recorder* 6 (1965): 4–13. Both articles obscure differences between tonguings mentioned in the sixteenth century, and those discussed in later times.

[3] Rogniono, bk. II, fol. C1ᵛ, explicitly says this, and the others imply that the simple tongue stroke was normal for longer notes. Ganassi, *Fontegara*, chap. 8, mentions still another method of articulating. He writes, 'trovarsi un altra lingua laquale non proferisse sillaba niuna & il moto suo sie da uno labro a l'altro & per occupar il fiato arente i lapri la si domanda lingua di testa', which might be paraphrased, 'there is another tonguing in which no syllable is pronounced, and the method of attack is by one lip or the other, and because the breath is controlled solely by the lips, it is called 'head articulation'. In other words, a note is attacked directly, without any tongue stroke. Horsley, 'Wind Techniques', p. 60, points out that this articulation is not described again until 1636, when Marin Mersenne mentions it.

alternately by the tongue and the throat. Modern double tonguing, 'te ke te ke' or 'de ke de ke', was too harsh for most sixteenth-century ears. Dalla Casa suggests that it be reserved for special effects, for those who wish to 'far terribiltà'.[1] The softest of these articulations, 'ler ler', or 'lere lere', Dalla Casa considered the normal one for *passaggi*, for he calls it 'lingua di gorgia', diminution tonguing. It is, in effect, a tongued legato which divides figuration patterns into groups of two notes each:

lere   lere   lere   lere

just different enough from a true legato to assure that each note in a fast passage be heard distinctly.[2] And, finally, there is an intermediate kind of articulation, 'terler terler', 'tere lere tere lere', 'derler derler', or 'dere lere dere lere', between the two extremes but combining elements of both, and it has the effect of dividing figuration patterns into groupings of four notes each:

tere   lere   tere   lere

In addition, Ganassi points out that both the consonant and the vowel sound can be changed in any one of the suggested combinations, so that in place of 'tere', for example, the player can substitute 'tara', 'tiri', 'toro', 'turu', or 'gara', 'ghere', 'ghiri', 'goro', 'guru', and so on.[3] But these

---

[1] Dalla Casa, bk. II, fol. 1ᵛ.

[2] This interpretation differs from the one in Houle, p. 7, which is based on the erroneous notion that '*le* is a weaker articulation than *re*', an idea apparently derived from a statement by Johann Joachim Quantz in 1752 about a different sort of double tonguing. But Dalla Casa's application of the 'lingua di gorgia' in his musical examples, pp. 1–2, as well as his terminology, makes it clear that he had in mind a 'tongued legato' grouped in twos, 'lé re lé re', and so on, which had to be fluent enough for use with hemidemisemiquavers as well as demisemiquavers. In fact, this tonguing helps the recorder player to perform fast passage work precisely and clearly, a virtue extolled by Rogniono, bk. II, fol. C1ᵛ, among others. A true legato on a mechanically simple wind instrument like the recorder is difficult for two reasons: the player must often move many fingers together because of cross-fingerings and such changes are virtually impossible to make simultaneously; and the player must often skip from fundamental to overtone and back again, not an easy feat to perform without the aid of some tongue stroke, however unobtrusive. Reversed tonguings help greatly in overcoming both difficulties.

[3] Ganassi, *Fontegara*, chap. 7.

refinements are a matter either of individual taste or of differences so subtle that they are lost to modern ears.

Wind players, then, normally tongued even the fastest notes of *passaggi*, albeit often with gentle and inconspicuous strokes. Dalla Casa, in fact, explicitly criticizes those players who slur *passaggi* because they are easier to perform that way, and reversed tonguings are difficult to control.[1] But some musicians, as Dalla Casa himself admits, did slur. And the technique was known to string as well as to wind players. While Ganassi in *Regola Rubertina* is ambiguous on this point, he did recognize the necessity of playing two or three consecutive down- or up-bows, mostly in order to make the weighted bow coincide with the accented beat, but he seems not to know the true legato.[2] So it was Ortiz who first mentioned it, when he suggested that two or three semiminims (quavers in the musical examples) could be taken in one bow.[3] As the speed and complexity of ornaments increased toward the end of the century, string players had more need of legato bowing, in order to play *passaggi* that moved too quickly for separate strokes, and in order to play accented notes with a weighted arm. By 1592, Rogniono regards grouping two or three notes under one bow as the normal procedure.[4]

Apparently, then, sixteenth-century instrumental music was usually performed entirely in a detached manner, with one bow- or tongue-stroke per note. The speed of improvised ornamentation, though, prompted players to enlarge their techniques to include slurred groupings, a device, we may imagine, that was soon adopted for reasons of musical variety as well as physical necessity. While the sixteenth-century string players offer no information about the way in which slurred notes were grouped, the nature of reversed tonguing suggests that figuration patterns were normally

arranged in twos or fours. Four semiquavers (*crome*),

---

[1] Dalla Casa, bk. II, fol. 1ᵛ.

[2] This point is developed at greater length in David D. Boyden, *The History of Violin Playing from Its Origins to 1761 and Its Relationship to the Violin and Violin Music* (London, 1965), pp. 77–84.

[3] Ortiz, p. 5, and, in German, p. xxix.

[4] Rogniono, bk. II, fol. C1ᵛ.

for example, should either be detached, played as one unit under a

single slur, , or divided into two groups of two notes

each, . And until new evidence comes to light, those

three ways of phrasing should be considered the most usual manner of playing the shorter notes of sixteenth-century music.

6

REACTIONS AGAINST
THE VIRTUOSO

A plausible conception of the nature and history of ornamentation can be gained from the information supplied by the various treatises. The impression that they are generally reliable is reinforced by the fact that the practical advice they offer is often sound and sensible. It therefore seems captious to believe that they do not reflect the true practice of their times. And yet Einstein writes that we should not be misled into believing that musicians actually performed the 'monstrosities' that appear as examples in some of these books.[1] But even if we agree with him that Rogniono, Bovicelli, and some of the others were guilty of barbarism and bad taste, we cannot use this value judgment as evidence that sixteenth-century performers never subverted the intentions of composers by piling on extravagant embellishments until the original composition was completely hidden from sound. Surely bad taste is not the exclusive property of the present century.

The enormous repertoire of lute and keyboard intabulations, many of them ornamented beyond any immediate recognition of the compositions they mask, furnishes abundant proof that sixteenth-century performers aggressively asserted their rights. The difference between a good and a bad intabulation hangs precisely on the skill with which the virtuoso embellished his model, and I daresay that most of the best ones transgress the limits of tolerance that we today would be inclined to set on freedom for the performer. The nature of this repertoire of instrumental arrangements, incidentally, strongly suggests that all genres of sixteenth-century composition, chansons, madrigals, villanelle, motets, *falsobordoni*, and even Mass Ordinaries, were capable of being treated in the same disrespectful manner,

[1] Einstein, *Italian Madrigal* 2: 840–42.

which is not to say that every sixteenth-century performer elaborately embellished all the compositions that he performed. On the contrary, I have tried to establish criteria for deciding which compositions were normally decorated and which were not. These criteria have more to do with the number and kinds of musicians than with the nature of the music. Thus, instrumentalists were apparently more inclined to improvise than singers. And both instrumental and vocal ensembles would have added rather discreet ornaments, intended simply to decorate, while solo virtuosi may in their narcissism often have destroyed the character of the music they performed by their excessive and flamboyant embellishments.

But we should not underestimate the liberty — some might call it licence — of the sixteenth-century performers in fleshing out what they considered the skeletons of scores provided by the composers. A madrigal, for example, might well have been performed as written, with one singer to a part and without instrumental doubling. But there is abundant evidence — and more of it appears the later in the century we look[1] — that, in theory at least, any such composition might also have been performed with instruments, or arranged for solo voice or instrument and lute, for two or three voices and lute, or for some other combination of voices and/ or instruments. Einstein would have us believe that only those madrigals that had self-contained top lines or particularly declamatory melodies were singled out for solo, that is, pseudo-monodic, performance; and he rightly points out that Willaert, for example, did not arrange all of Verdelot's madrigals for voice and lute, but only those that are stylistically most suitable.[2] But he is really only praising Willaert for being an unusually sensitive musician. All madrigals could have been and doubtless were arranged as solos or duets; but some were more adaptable than others.

The truth is that virtuosi, both singers and instrumentalists, did exist in the sixteenth century; they did arrange all sorts of compositions for solo

---

[1] See, for example, the two volumes published by Emanuel Adriansen, listed in Brown, *Instrumental Music*, as 1584₆ and 1592₆, which contain polyphonic compositions, mostly madrigals, arranged in such a way that they can be performed by varying combinations of lutes and voices.

[2] Einstein, *Italian Madrigal*, 1: 227, 2: 840–42.

performance; and doubtless some, and perhaps many, exhibited execrable taste in so doing. Einstein is indubitably correct in insisting on the fundamental incompatibility of composer and virtuoso, and on the basic conflict between expression and ornamentation. And a number of the most serious musicians of the sixteenth century agreed with him. According to an anecdote, probably apocryphal since it was first reported in 1562, Josquin des Prez did not tolerate embellishments. When he heard a singer ornamenting one of his compositions, he went up to him and said: 'You ass, why do you add embellishments? If I had wanted them, I would have written them myself. If you wish to improve on finished compositions, make your own, but leave mine unimproved.'[1] Juan Bermudo warned beginning keyboard players never to play from tablatures already prepared, because they were all filled with mistakes, by which he almost certainly meant excessive decoration.[2] Gioseffo Zarlino sharply criticizes singers who apply diminutions which are wild and out of proportion, disturb the listeners, and create many errors.[3] And Ercole Bottrigari considers *passaggi* one of the chief causes of discord and confusion in the performances which he was attacking.[4] In short, there was strong disagreement in the sixteenth century about the effectiveness of improvised ornamentation, and it is this disagreement along with the existence of flamboyant examples in the embellishment manuals that forces us to conclude that Einstein is wrong in writing that 'there was not yet that abuse of freedom that characterized the beginning of the seventeenth century and whose correction required the century's untiring efforts.'[5] For it was precisely during the late sixteenth century that such abuses of freedom flourished unchecked. Indeed, the ultimate triumph and justification of improvised ornamentation was the role it played in transforming the music of the Renaissance into something new and essentially different.

---

[1] Reported in Helmuth Osthoff, *Josquin Desprez* (Tutzing, 1962) 1: 82.

[2] *Instrumentos musicales*, bk. IV, chap. 1, fol. 60, and see also chap. 43, fols. 84ᵛ–85.

[3] *Istitutioni harmoniche* (Venice, 1558; facsimile of the 1573 ed., 1966), part III, chap. 46, pp. 239–40. The passage is quoted and translated in Einstein, *Italian Madrigal* 2: 842–43.

[4] *Il Desiderio* (Venice, 1594) facsimile ed., by Kathi Meyer (1924), pp. 50–51, and, in English translation by Carol MacClintock (American Institute of Musicology, 1962), p. 61.

[5] Einstein, *Italian Madrigal* 2: 843.

Giulio Caccini's monodies[1] look more highly decorated than most late sixteenth-century madrigals. Their appearance is deceptive, however, for they probably sounded simpler in performance than most polyphonic madrigals that were arranged as solos and embellished. Caccini, in other words, made an earnest effort to compose all the ornamentation that had hitherto been improvised in an attempt to control the amount and kind of it and to reconcile the two extremes, expression and ornamentation. Similarly, the new style of Monteverdi's later madrigals, from his fifth book onwards, results at least partly from his desire to incorporate the florid counterpoint of improvising virtuosi into his music as an integral part of the melodic structure.[2] Throughout the sixteenth century virtuosi arranged, or perhaps it would be better to say, disarranged, polyphonic music to suit their own slightly suspect artistic purposes. Gradually composers began to take these virtuosi into account in planning their pieces: Luzzaschi's madrigals for the three ladies of Ferrara are perhaps the best-known examples of this sort of accommodation.[3] And finally the practice of improvising ornamentation helped to transform musical style altogether, as the Renaissance came to an end and the Baroque era began.

[1] *Le nuove musiche* (Florence, 1601). Some of the monodies published with ornamentation in this volume appear in unadorned versions in St. Michael's College, Tenbury, MS 1018; see Nancy Maze, 'Tenbury MS 1018: A Key to Caccini's Art of Embellishment', *Journal of the American Musicological Society* 9 (1956): 61–63. Similarly some English seventeenth-century songs exist in both plain and ornamented versions; see Nigel Fortune, 'Solo Song and Cantata', *New Oxford History of Music*, vol. 4: *The Age of Humanism, 1540–1630*, ed. Gerald Abraham (London, 1968), pp. 215–17.

[2] On this point see Claude Palisca, 'The Artusi-Monteverdi Controversy', in *The Monteverdi Companion*, ed. Denis Arnold and Nigel Fortune (London, 1968), esp. pp. 136–42.

[3] See Kinkeldey, *Orgel und Klavier*, pp. 157 ff., and Einstein, *Italian Madrigal* 2: 834–35.

INDEX OF NAMES